True Worship

by Billy W. Moore

"God is a Spirit: and they that worship Him must worship Him in spirit and truth."

—John 4:24

ONE STONE
BIBLICAL RESOURCES

Published by:
One Stone Press
979 Lovers Lane
Bowling Green, KY 42103

Printed in the United States of America

ISBN 10: 978-1-941422-69-4

www.onestone.com

To my father, Carl Moore, and the memory of my mother, Lillie Howell Moore, who taught me how to worship God "in spirit and in truth."

Acknowledgments

It is impossible for me to know all the sources from which the material in this book has been gleaned. I am indebted to a host of people. Whenever possible I have given credit. I am grateful to our Father in heaven for the blessings and opportunities that have been mine and for the influence of godly men and women in my life.

I must give a special acknowledgment to my son, Terry, for the many hours he has spent in typing copy for this book. Thus, to him I am especially grateful. Also, to my wife, Dee, for the help she has been in proof reading, corrections and suggestions for layout.

Most of all I am indebted to God who has given me "life, and breath, and all things" necessary for life in this world. May this book bring glory and honor unto him.

— *The Author*

Introduction

Throughout the centuries the people of God have worshipped Him. In preceding ages, the worship differed from Christian worship, but nonetheless it showed respect and reverence for God as the creator of man and the giver of life.

"God is greatly to be feared in the assembly of the saints, and to be had in reverence of all them that are about him." (Psalm 89:7) When the saints of God meet for worship, there should be an attitude of reverence and a sense of respect prevailing in the assembly. It is not to do our own bidding that we assemble, but to praise and honor the true and living God, and our Lord and Savior Jesus Christ.

In the assemblies of the saints, "Let all things be done decently and in order" (1 Corinthians 14:40). Speaking of things decent, Alexander Campbell wrote, "...may we not infer that even the dress of Christians in the public assembly is either decent or indecent, according to the standard of Christian simplicity and decorum? If this be true of a Christian's dress, it is equally true of his manners. The dress and manners of God's house ought not to be after the model of the dress and the manners of the forum, the theatre, or the carousals of a public entertainment." (*Millennial Harbinger*, 1835, p. 507, as quoted in the *Pioneers On Worship* by John Allen Hudson, page 64.)

There is a definite order of Christian worship. In the words of A. Campbell, "By the phrase, 'order of Christian worship,' we do not mean the position of the bodies of the worshippers, not the hour of the day in which certain things are to be done, nor whether one action shall be always performed first, another always second, and another always third...but there are certain social acts of Christian worship, all of which are to be attended to in the Christian assembly, and each of which is essential to the perfection of the whole as every member of the human body is essential to the perfect man—is that which we wish to convey by the phrase 'order of Christian worship'" (Ibid., pages 57-58).

In this series of lessons we shall study worship and the acts of Christian worship as taught in the New Testament, with the hope that such a study shall help us to better worship our God "in spirit and in truth." Realizing that we belong to God, body and spirit, and that we are to glorify and praise Him on the earth, may we, like the Psalmist of old say,

"I will sing unto the Lord as long as I live:
I will sing praise to my God while I have my being" (Psalm 104:33).

How to Use This Book

This book directs the student to the Word of God. There are hundreds of scripture references in these lessons which must be read and studied with care in order to answer the questions that are asked. On preparing these lessons the King James Version was used, unless otherwise stated. It may be of profit to compare other versions. The student should never try to get a lesson without reading the scripture references.

The lessons are designed to help the student come to a better understanding of true worship, what it is and the different acts in which the children of God engage when they worship Him "in spirit and in truth."

The lessons are arranged so that one lesson period is used on an outline (in some instances two weeks may be required for this), studying the outline, reading the scripture references and trying to compress each student with the points that are made. (Members of the class may be asked to give a brief report on a particular point in an outline. If this is done the teacher must make assignments in advance.) The next lesson period is devoted to the questions and answers. In this session the students will have greater participation in the class, while the teacher leads the class and promotes further discussion that may be needed. The material in this book is sufficient for at least eighteen lessons.

Remember: the purpose of this series of lessons is to teach the Word of God as it relates to the subject of true worship, and to emphasize the importance of Christians worshipping God as He desires that we may be acceptable in His sight.

Table of Contents

A Study of Worship

INTRODUCTION

1. Define worship:

    a. Joseph H. Thayer: *proskuneo*—"to kiss the hand to (towards) one, in token of reverence...hence among the Orientals, esp. the Persians, to fall upon the knees and touch the ground with the forehead as an expression of profound reverence... hence in the N.T., by kneeling or prostration to do homage (to one) or make obeisance, whether in order to express respect or to make supplication. It is used a. of homage shown to men of superior rank...b. of homage rendered to God and the ascended Christ, to heavenly beings, and to demons..." (*Greek-English Lexicon*)

    b. W. E. Vine: "*proskuneo* to make obeisance, do reverence to (from *pros*, towards, and *kuneo*, to kiss), is the most frequent word rendered worship. It is used of homage or reverence (a) to God...(b) to Christ...(c) to a man...(d) to the Dragon...(e) to the Beast...(f) the image of the beast...(g) to demons... (h) to idols..." Four other Greek words which are translated worship are also mentioned, B.M., then Mr. Vine makes the following notes:

        NOTES: (1) The worship of God is nowhere defined in Scripture. A consideration of the above verbs shows that it is not confined to praise; broadly it may be regarded as the direct acknowledgment to God, of his nature, attributes, ways and claims, whether by the outgoing of the heart in praise and thanksgiving or by deeds done in such acknowledgment. (2) In Acts 17:25 *therapeuo*, to serve, do service (so R.V.) is rendered 'is worshipped'" (*An Expository Dictionary of New Testament Words*).

    c. The best simple definition for worship is, the expression of the adoration of one's heart.

2. The use of the word "worship" in the Old Testament. Robert Young lists 116 times the word is used in the Old Testament (see *Young's Analytical Concordance*).

a. It is most frequently translated from the Hebrew word *shachah*, which means "to bow self down" (99 times).*

  (1) This same word is translated "bow down" (9), "bow down selves" (8), "bow selves" (35), "do obeisance" (5), "fall down" (3), "fall flat" (91), "humbly beseech" (1), "make obeisance" (4).

  (2) This helps one understand the true meaning of the word *shachah*, which is so frequently translated worship.

b. *Segab* is translated "worship" 11 times—"to bow down, do obeisance" (Daniel 2, 3).

c. *Abad* (5 times in 2 Kings 10) "to do, serve."

d. *Atsab* (1 time, Jeremiah 44:19) "to make an idol."

3. The word worship is found 76* times in the New Testament.

a. Most frequently from the Greek *proskuneo*, "to kiss the hand to (towards) in token of reverence" (59 times).

b. It is found 17 other times, from ten different words (see *Young's Analytical Concordance*).

  (1) "Glory" (1), Luke 14:10

  (2) "To be reverential, pious" (1), Acts 17:23

  (3) "To serve, cure, heal" (1), Acts 17:25

  (4) "Religious observance (1), Colossians 2:18

  (5) "To worship publicly" (4)

  (6) "A temple sweeper" (1)

  (7) "A worshipper" (1), John 4:23

  (8) "To venerate" (6)

  (9) "An object of veneration" (1)

  (10) "Worshipper" one who venerates God (1), John 9:31

I. Man is a creature of worship. By nature he will worship someone or something.

A. Since we are the "offspring of God" (Acts 17:29), he is the "Father of our spirits," therefore, he has the right to direct us in our worship.

  1. We can know the mind of God only as he has revealed himself to man (1 Corinthians 2:11-13).

* The numbers in ( ) indicate the number of times that word is found.

2. In his word God teaches man how to worship.

    a. To worship in any way not taught in his word is to be presumptuous. How can we know that God will be pleased with our worship if he has not told us that such worship pleases him?

B. It should be noted that some worship is not pleasing or acceptable unto God.

    1. Jesus said to the woman at the well, "Ye worship ye know not what..." (John 4:22). Was this pleasing unto God?

    2. "In vain ye do worship me..." (Matthew 15:9)

    3. "...worshipped and served the creature more than the creator" (Romans 1:25).

    4. "...whom ye ignorantly worship" (Acts 17:23).

    5. The Jews understood that one's worship could be wrong. "This fellow persuadeth men to worship God contrary to the law" (Acts 18:13).

    6. "All Asia and the world worshippeth Diana, the goddess" (Acts 19:27).

    7. "Which things have indeed a shew of wisdom in will worship..." (Colossians 2:23)
        Note: These references surely warrant the following conclusions.

        a. One may worship and still be wrong.

        b. One may worship the one true God and still be wrong.

        c. There are different kinds of worship. In the following point we shall study each of these.

II. There are different kinds of worship.
     Note: While one may list each kind of worship separately, I believe all kinds of worship may properly be listed under two headings, i.e. true and false worship.

A. True worship—acceptable worship (John 4:23, 24)

    1. True worship will be directed unto God and will be rendered in spirit and in truth.

        a. Further study will be given to these points when we study the requirements of true worship.

B. False worship—unacceptable worship (John 4:23, 24)
Note: False is the opposite of true, unacceptable the opposite of acceptable. So, if one could have a true worship he could also have a false worship.

1. Vain worship (Matthew 15:9)

    a. Jesus taught that the Jews were worshipping in vain because they were "teaching for doctrine the commandments of men."

        (1) They directed their worship unto God, but they taught the doctrines of men and this made their worship vain (empty, not yielding the desired outcome).

        (2) It did not matter that their worship was directed unto the true God, this was not sufficient to make it acceptable.

    b. Men today who worship God but who use for doctrine the commandments of men cannot expect to render true—acceptable—worship. Their worship will be just as vain as that of the Jews.

2. Ignorant worship (Acts 17:23)

    a. Those of Athens worshipped the true God, but they worshipped him in ignorance.

        (1) They bowed down before an image with the inscription "to the Unknown God." The only true God was unknown to them, but he cannot be worshipped acceptably in ignorance.

    b. Note: Ignorant worship is "in vain," but all vain worship may not be done in ignorance. Some may know that their worship is after the doctrines of men but may be too proud to change. Though they are not ignorant of truth, their worship is nonetheless in vain.

3. Will-worship (Colossians 2:23)

    a. "Voluntarily adopted worship, whether unbidden or forbidden, not that which is imposed by others, but which one affects" (W.E. Vine).

    b. "Will-worship is after our own will. It is self-chosen; and for this single reason is a departure from allegiance to God" (David Lipscomb, *A Commentary on The New Testament, Vol. IV,* page 287).

c. "However plausible and specious such worship may appear, however much of show of wisdom it may exhibit, the Holy Spirit has written its folly and emptiness so plainly that none but the willingly blind can fail to see it. Loyalty to the divine government requires hearty obedience to divine law. Whatever God commands, therefore, we must do. To hesitate is to falter, is to forsake our allegiance. To set up any 'commandment of men,' and honor it as a command of God, is treason. God's will is expressed in his commandments. Every commandment, even the least, is an expression of his will, and an embodiment of his authority as the monarch of the universe. To obey his commandment, to do his will, is, therefore, the very essence of true piety. Everything else is mere will-worship" (J.W. Shepherd, ibid., page 287).

d. "What is here termed will-worship...signifies simply a mode of worship which a man choses for himself, independently of the revelation which God has given...God will be served in his own way; it is right that he should prescribe to man the truths which he is to believe, and the ordinances which he is to use. To refuse to receive his teaching in order to prefer our own fancies, is to light a farthing candle as a substitute for the noonday sun. From the beginning of the world God has prescribed the worship which was best pleasing to himself, and never left a matter of such moment [importance] to man. The nations which have either not had a revelation, or refused to receive that which God has given, show, by their diversity of worship, superstition, absurdity, and in many cases cruelty, what the state of the whole would have been, had not God, in his infinite mercy, blessed it with a revelation of his will"—Adam Clarke (*Clarke's Commentary, Vol. VI*, page 525).

e. We conclude that will-worship is a worship which one designs himself. All will-worship is false; it is vain. It may be done in ignorance, but one could follow will-worship without being in ignorance.

III.   True worship requires three things.

A. The proper object

1. The one true and living God is the proper object of worship (John 4:23-24). Reasons why man should worship God:

   a. God desires that men worship him. "...for the Father seeketh such to worship him" (John 4:23).

   b. Because he is the "one God and Father of all, who is above all, and through all, and in you all" (Ephesians 4:6).

      (1) We are his "offspring" (Acts 17:29), he had made men to dwell on the earth (Acts 17:26), "in him we live, and move, and have our being" (Acts 17:28), "every good gift and every perfect gift is from above, and cometh down from the Father of lights..." (James 1:17).

   c. Jesus said, "Thou shalt worship the Lord they God, and him only shalt thou serve" (Matthew 4:10).

   d. Jesus allowed men to worship him.
      Note: Jesus is God (deity), and during his life among men he accepted worship.

      (1) The wise men worshipped him (Matthew 2:1).

      (2) A leper worshipped him (Matthew 8:2).

      (3) A ruler worshipped him (Matthew 9:18).

      (4) His disciples worshipped him (Matthew 14:33).

      (5) The woman of Canaan worshipped him (Matthew 15:25).

      (6) The mother of Zebedee's children worshipped him (Matthew 28:10).

      (7) The women who had gone to the tomb worshipped him (Matthew 28:10).

      (8) The eleven disciples worshipped him (Matthew 28:17).

      (9) The blind man whom Jesus healed worshipped him (John 9:38).

      But Jesus taught men to worship the Father in Heaven (John 4:23, 24).

2. Other objects of worship

   a. Other men

      (1) Cornelius fell at Peter's feet to worship him (Acts 10:25, 26).

(2) The people of Lystra sought to worship Paul and Barnabas (Acts 14:8-18).

(3) Some men desire that other men worship them (2 Thessalonians 2:3-4).

b. Angels

(1) John fell at the feet of the angel to worship (Revelation 22:9-10).

(2) Worshipping of angels can beguile men (Colossians 2:18).

c. Idols—these are gods made with the hands of men

(1) Those of Athens worshipped many idols (Acts 17:16).

(2) Idolatry was common in Old Testament times, and even the children of Israel made idols.

(a) Moloch and Remphan, "figures which ye made to worship them" (Acts 7:43)

(3) Some interesting things about this kind of god:

(a) Men make them with their hands.

(b) They bear him upon the shoulder, they carry him.

(c) They set him in his place, and he standeth; for his place shall he not remove.

(d) One shall cry unto him, yet can he not answer, nor save him out of his trouble.
Question: Why would men want to worship a god like that?

(4) Notice what Elijah had to say about this kind of a god (1 Kings 18:27).

(a) Maybe he can't hear you because he is talking to someone else; or he is pursuing, or on a journey and can not be reached; or he is asleep and you can not wake him.

(b) Would you want to serve a god like that?

d. The creatures of this world (Romans 1:25)

(1) Many people in ancient times as well as modern times worship the cow and consider it a sacred animal.

(2) While in Nigeria, I learned of a tribe that worships snakes, the giant pythons and boa constrictors. They keep them in their huts, pet them, feed them, and when one of those snakes dies they provide an elaborate funeral for it.

e.   The devil (Matthew 4:9)

(1) The devil desires worship, and he gets it. The church of the devil was established by Anton Szandor Levay, and their official creed is the Satanic Bible, written by Levay.

Note: It may be of interest to have someone give a special report on "The Church of the Devil."

Note: All true worship—acceptable worship—must be rendered unto God, who is the Father of all.

B.   True worship must be offered "in spirit" (John 4:23, 24)

1.   This has reference to sincerity, to the condition of one's mind when he worships.

"In spirit. The word spirit, here, stands opposed to rites and ceremonies, and to the pomp of external worship. It refers to the mind, the souls, the heart. They shall worship God with a sincere mind, with the simple offering of gratitude and prayer, with a desire to glorify him, and without external pomp and splendor. Spiritual worship is that where the heart is offered to God and where we do not depend on external forms for acceptance" (Albert Barnes, *Notes on the New Testament*, comment on John 4:23).

2.   Insincere worship is never acceptable even though it may be offered unto the one true God. It is always false worship.

3.   Worshipping God is a very serious matter and should not be engaged in lightly.

a.   For such a serious matter, we should be on time and prepare ourselves for the worship. To arrive late will interfere with the worship others are rendering, and will rob you of some time of worship.

b.   "God is greatly to be feared in the assembly of the saints, and to be had in reverence of all them that are about him" (Psalm 89:7).

      4. "In spirit" has to do with attitude and manners which we show in worship.

          a. The sincere person gives undivided attention to the speaker and through discipline has trained himself to think on what he is doing. He shows respect and reverence to God, and leaves feeling uplifted by having worshipped God.

  C. True worship must be offered "in truth" (John 4:23, 24)

      1. "In truth. Not through the medium of shadows and types, not by means of sacrifices and bloody offerings, but in the manner represented or typified by all of these, he. Lx. 9, 24 In the true way of direct access to God through Jesus Christ" (Albert Barnes, ibid.).

      2. "In truth" is used in contrast to "the law." "For the law was given by Moses, but grace and truth came by Jesus Christ" (John 1:17).

          a. This means we must worship as the New Testament teaches, not as the law of Moses taught. Going back to the law to justify a practice will make Christ become of none effect unto us (Galatians 5:4).

          b. Every act of true worship will be taught in the New Testament. To use in our worship that which is not authorized in the New Testament is to cease to practice true worship.

              (1) If our worship is not authorized in the New Testament, it must either come from the Old Testament, or it will be authorized only by men. Either way it will not be true worship.

          c. This explains why members of the churches of Christ insist that we worship only as the New Testament teaches.

IV.   How to worship God in spirit and in truth.

  A. There are five acts, or avenues, of true worship (cf. Acts 2:42).

      1. Apostles' doctrine (the teaching given by the apostles)

      2. Breaking of bread, or the Lord's Supper

      3. Fellowship, or laying by in store

      4. Prayers

      5. Singing songs of praise (Ephesians 5:19; Colossians 3:16)

    B.   These acts of worship must be rendered "in spirit and in truth."

        1.   This means we must always be sincere when we worship, and each act of worship must be as the New Testament teaches.

        2.   The truth restricts some of these acts to be done only "upon the first day of the week."

            a.   The Lord's Supper (Acts 20:7)

            b.   Laying by in store (1 Corinthians 16:1-2)

CONCLUSION

1.   We shall study each act of Christian worship in lessons to follow.

2.   May we recognize the importance of worshipping God, and may our worship be true worship.

Some Questions on Worship

WHAT DOES THE SCRIPTURE SAY?

References: Matthew 4:10; John 4:24; Matthew 15:9; Romans 1:25;
Acts 17:23; Acts 18:13; Colossians 2:23; Acts 10:25-26; Revelation 22:18-19;
Isaiah 46:5-6

1. "Thou shalt _____ the Lord thy _____, and him only shalt
    thou _____."

2. "God is a _____; and they that _____ him must
    _____ him in _____ and in _____."

3. "But in _____ they do _____ me, teaching for doctrines
    the _____ of men."

4. "Who changed the truth of God into a lie, and _____ and
    served the _____ more than the Creator, who is blessed for
    ever."

5. "For as I passed by and beheld your devotions, I found an altar with
    this inscription, _____ _____ _____ _____. Whom
    therefore ye _____ worship."

6. "This fellow persuadeth men to _____ God contrary to
    the _____."

7. "Which things have indeed a show of wisdom in _____
    _____, and humility, and neglecting of the body not in
    any honor to the satisfying of the flesh."

8. "And as Peter was coming in, Cornelius met him, and fell down at
    his feet, and _____ him. But Peter took him up saying,
    _____ up; I myself also am a man."

9.   "If any man _____ unto these things, God shall _____ unto him the _____ that are written in this book; and if any man shall _____ away from the words of this prophecy, God shall take away his _____ out of the _____ of _____ and out of the holy city."

10.   "To whom will ye _____ me, and make me equal, and _____ me, that we may be like?"

TALK TIME—DISCUSSION

1.   Study the definition of worship given in the introduction and be prepared to discuss it with the class.

   a.   Is it used only with reference to God? _____

   b.   Name others of whom this word is used. _____
   _____

2.   After reading Acts 17:29 and 1 Corinthians 2:11-13, you should be able to answer the following questions:

   a.   List two reasons why God has the right to direct our worship.

   (1) _____

   (2) _____

   b.   How can we know that our worship is acceptable to God?
   _____

   c.   Where may we learn how to worship God? _____

3.   Some worship is not acceptable unto God. Read the following passages and tell something about the worship mentioned in each of them.

   a.   John 4:22 _____

   b.   Matthew 15:9 _____

    c.   Romans 1:25 _____

    d.   Acts 17:23 _____

    e.   Acts 18:13 _____

    f.   Acts 19:27 _____

    g.   Colossians 2:23_____

4.   From the seven references studied in the preceding question, you should have a definite and firm answer for the following statements (yes or no—true or false).

    a.   One may worship and still be wrong. _____

    b.   One may worship the one true God and still be wrong._____

    c.   There are different kinds of worship. _____

5.   Subject: Kinds of worship

    a.   All worship may be classified into one of two kinds of worship. Name these two kinds.

        (1) _____

        (2) _____

6.   Under the heading of false worship—unacceptable worship—list three kinds of worship (cite a reference for each).

    a.   _____

    b.   _____

    c.   _____

7.   Subject: Vain worship

    a.   What is vain? _____

    b.   What made the worship of the Jews vain (Matthew 15:9)?

        _____

    c.   Would the same thing make our worship vain? _____

    d. Give at least two examples of vain worship. _____

_____

8.   Discuss ignorant worship.

    a. Define ignorant._____

    b. Whom did those of Athens worship ignorantly?_____

_____

    c. How did they worship God ignorantly?_____

_____

    d. Is ignorant worship in vain? _____ Is all vain worship done in ignorance? _____ Be prepared to show the line of difference between ignorant worship and vain worship. _____

_____

9.   Read Colossians 2:23 and some comments made on this passage. Then define will-worship.

    a. Will-worship is _____

_____

    b. Is will-worship always false? _____ Vain? _____ Is it always done in ignorance? _____

    c. What did David Lipscomb say about will-worship? It is a

_____ _____ _____ _____

Do you agree?_____

    d. Read J. W. Shepherd's comment on will-worship and answer the following:

      (1) To hesitate to obey God's command is _____

_____

      (2) To set up any "commandment of men" and honor it as a "command of God" is _____

      (3) To obey His commandment is _____

_____

e. What comparison did Adam Clarke use of those who would refuse God's teaching in order to prefer our own? _____

_____

10. True worship requires three things. Name them.

a. _____

b. _____

c. _____

11. Subject: the proper object of worship

a. Who is the object of true Worship?_____

b. Give three reasons why men should worship God.

(1) _____

(2) _____

(3) _____

c. Did Jesus allow men to worship him? _____ Give three examples:

(1) _____

(2) _____

(3) _____

d. Whom did Jesus teach men to worship?_____

12. The wrong object of worship

a. List five objects of worship and give a reference for each.

(1) _____

(2) _____

(3) _____

(4) _____

(5) _____

    b. What would cause one to worship a fellow man? _____

        _____

    c. How do we know that it is wrong to worship angels?_____

        _____

    d. What are idols?_____

        _____

    e. List four things about this kind of god (idols).

        (1) _____

        (2) _____

        (3) _____

        (4) _____

    f. What did Elijah mockingly say about this kind of god? _____

        _____

        _____

    g. Name some creatures of this world that men worship. _____

        _____

    h. Are there some who really worship the devil? _____
        Does he want men to worship him? _____
        (Note to the teacher: give a brief report on "The Church of the
        Devil" or have someone prepare it for the class.)

13. Discuss true worship

    a. True worship must be rendered in _____ and in

        _____.

    b. What does "in spirit" mean?_____

    c. What does "in truth" mean? _____

14. List the five acts of worship which may be offered in truth.

    a. _____

    b. _____

c. _____

d. _____

e. _____

THINK! "THINK ON THESE THINGS"

1. Jesus said, "Thou shalt worship the Lord thy God and him only shalt thou serve" (Matthew 4:10). Does this mean it is wrong for us to worship anybody else? THINK! _____

2. What about bowing before an image if we say we are not worshipping the image, but that which it reminds us of? Is this wrong? THINK! _____

3. Jesus said, "Those who worship God must worship him in spirit and in truth" (John 4:24). Is it possible for us to worship him otherwise? THINK!_____

4. Could we worship in spirit but not in truth? THINK! _____
   How could this be done? THINK! _____

   _____

5. Could we worship in truth but not in spirit? THINK! _____
   How could this be done? _____

   _____

6. Is it proper to conclude that anyone who worships God with a sincere heart is pleasing unto God? THINK! _____

7. Would you as soon worship a god made with men's hands as to worship the God who made man? THINK!_____

8. Do you have friends who may be worshipping in vain? THINK! _____

9. What can we do to help more people worship God acceptably?____

   _____

10.   Is one showing sincerity in worship when he frequently forsakes the hours of worship? THINK! _____

11.   Can one be saved eternally if he does not worship God in spirit and in truth? THINK! _____
      Should this make worship an important thing in the lives of God's people? THINK! _____

12.   After studying this lesson on worship can you say, "I have been doing my best," or do you see room for improvement? THINK!
      _____

 MEMORY—"THY WORD HAVE I HID IN MINE HEART"

1.   "Thou shalt worship the Lord thy God, and him only shalt thou serve" (Matthew 4:10).

2.   "God is a Spirit, and they that worship him must worship him in spirit and in truth" (John 4:24).

3.   "God is greatly to be feared in the assembly of the saints" (Psalm 89:7).

The Apostles' Doctrine

INTRODUCTION

1. Before Jesus ascended into heaven he charged the apostles to preach the gospel, to teach all nations, and to baptize the believers (Matthew 28:18-19 and Mark 16:15-16). The work of the apostles did not end when they baptized people. They were commanded to teach those who had been baptized "to observe all things whatsoever I have commanded you" (Matthew 28:20).

2. On the day of Pentecost (Acts 2) about three thousand souls were baptized in the name of Christ. Of these souls it is said, "And they continued steadfastly in the apostles' doctrine" (Acts 2:42). The apostles were teaching them the will of the Lord so they would not be "tossed to and fro...with every wind of doctrine" (Ephesians 4:14).

3. In this lesson we shall study "the apostles' doctrine."

I. What is the apostles' doctrine?

   A. Doctrine is teaching.

      1. Revised Version reads "apostles' teaching."

      2. Some were teaching for doctrine the commandments of men (Matthew 15:9).

      3. There are references in the scriptures to:

         a. Doctrines of men (Colossians 2:22)

         b. Doctrines of devils (1 Timothy 4:1)

         c. The doctrine of God ("adorn the doctrine of God," Titus 2:10)

         d. The doctrine of Christ (Mark 1:22; 4:2; 11:18; 12:38)

         e. Apostles' doctrine

   B. Apostles' doctrine is the teaching of the apostles.

      1. The doctrine did not originate with them.

         a. Jesus said, "My doctrine is not mine, but his that sent me" (John 7:16).

      b.   Even so, the apostles' doctrine is not their own but his that sent them.

    2.   It was called the apostles' doctrine because they preached it.

      a.   Cf. Acts 5:28: "ye have filled Jerusalem with your doctrine."

      b.   But they preached the doctrine of the Lord (Acts 13:12).

      c.   It was a "new doctrine" for it was first preached by the apostles (Acts 17:19).

      d.   It is "good doctrine" (1 Timothy 4:6).

C.   The apostles' doctrine was the word which they preached.

    1.   Paul charged Timothy to "preach the word...exhort with all longsuffering and doctrine" (2 Timothy 4:2).

D.   The apostles' doctrine is sound doctrine.

    1.   Cf. 1 Timothy 1:10; 2 Timothy 4:3; Titus 1:9; 2:1

E.   The apostles' doctrine is "the faith."

    1.   Called the "words of faith" (1 Timothy 4:6).

      a.   Note: R. V. reads "nourished in the words of the faith."

    2.   There is "one faith" (Ephesians 4:4-5), the teaching of Christ, the New Testament.

    3.   Note: The Law of Moses did not originate with Moses but is so called because it was spoken and written by Moses. So the "apostles' doctrine" did not originate with them but is so called because it was preached and written by the apostles.

II.   The apostles' doctrine came by revelation (Galatians 1:10-11).

A.   Jesus taught them during His personal ministry.

    1.   "I have given unto them the words which thou gavest me..." (John 17:8).

    2.   They were not able to receive all his teaching (John 16:7-12).

B.   Jesus promised to send the Holy Spirit unto them.

    1.   When He came he was to:

      a.   "Bring to remembrance all things I have taught you" (John 14:26).

      b.   "Teach you all things" (John 14:26).

    c. "Testify of me" (John 15:26).

    d. "Guide you into all truth" (John 16:13).
Note: This is the baptism of the Holy Spirit which they received on Pentecost (Acts 2:1-4).

2. Jesus said, "Take no thought how or what ye shall speak" (Matthew 10:19).

    a. Why? "It shall be given you in that same hour what ye shall speak."

    b. This is inspiration (Matthew 10:20).

3. They spoke the very words which they received of the Spirit (1 Corinthians 2:9-12).

    a. Note: The Spirit received them from God (John 16:13). Therefore, the apostles' doctrine is the word of God (Cf. 1 Corinthians 14:37).

C. The apostles' were to be "witnesses," "ambassadors," "chosen vessels," and "earthen vessels."

1. As witnesses they testified of things they had seen and heard (Luke 24:28; Acts 1:8; 2:32; 5:32).

    a. Peter said we "were eyewitnesses" (2 Peter 1:16).

    b. Matthias was chosen "to be a witness" (Acts 1:22).

    c. The Lord appeared to Saul to make him a witness (Acts 26:16).

2. As ambassadors, they were authorized to represent Christ (2 Corinthians 5:20)

3. As chosen vessels and earthen vessels they were the chosen men in which the truth would be placed (Acts 9:15).

    a. Gideon's men and their earthen vessels serve as a shadow or figure of the message being first in men, earthen vessels (Judges 7:15-23).
Note: The Holy Spirit came to enable them to serve in this mission.

III. The apostles' doctrine was written.

A. It was first all in men—inspired men.

1. A few years from Pentecost before any of it was written

B. Then it was in men and in epistles (written).

       1.   Early church was taught by word and epistle (2 Thessalonians 2:15).

       2.   Thus, part in men and part in written form.

   C. All truth was written before the close of the first century A.D.

       1.   They wrote the commandments of God (1 Corinthians 14:37).

       2.   They wrote all the truth (Acts 20:27; 1 Peter 1:3; John 20:20, 31).

       3.   We must not think of men above that which is written (1 Corinthians 4:6).

IV.   The nature of the apostles' doctrine.

   A. It is divine.

       1.   Hence, the word of God and not of men (1 Thessalonians 2:13; 2 Thessalonians 2:10, 11)

   B. It is complete.

       1.   Guided into all truth (John 16:13)

       2.   Furnishes us unto every good work (2 Timothy 3:16, 17)

   C. It is final (Jude 3).

       1.   Once delivered (Hebrews 9:27, 24-26)

       2.   Thus, no latter day revelations.

   D. It is authoritative (Matthew 16:19; Acts 15)

       1.   Withdraw from those who teach another doctrine (1 Thessalonians 3:14; 1 Timothy 6:3-5).

       2.   Those who transgress this doctrine have not God (2 John 9-10).

       3.   Do not think of men above what is written (1 Corinthians 4:6). Note: It should be the means of settling every difference (1 Peter 4:11).

   E. It is a message (doctrine) of salvation (Romans 1:16).

       1.   To be preached to every creature (Mark 16:16).

       2.   One must obey a "form" of that doctrine to be saved (Romans 6:16-18).

V.   The importance of continuing in the apostles' doctrine.

   A. The apostles were to teach those who believed and were baptized to observe all things Jesus commanded (Matthew 28:19-20).

      1. When they taught these things their teachings were called "the apostles' doctrine."

      2. The early disciples "continued steadfastly in the apostles' doctrine" (Acts 2:42).

  B. We must continue in this doctrine to be saved (1 Timothy 4:16).

      1. Man or angel is condemned if he teaches another gospel (doctrine) (Galatians 1:6-12).

      2. Those who transgress the doctrine are without God (2 John 9-11).

      3. The Lord said, "Be thou faithful unto death..." (Revelation 2:10).

  C. Elders are to see that the apostles' doctrine is taught in the local church.

      1. "Feed the flock of God which is among you..." (1 Peter 5:2; Acts 20:28).

      2. They must "be able by sound doctrine both to convince and exhort the gainsayers" (Titus 1:9).
Note: Regarding this doctrine we should notice several things:

         a. It is not "our" doctrine.

         b. It is not "my" doctrine.

         c. It is not the church's doctrine.

            (1) Some churches are governed by a body of men called a synod, council, conference, etc. This body has the right to legislate to the church, so they make "church doctrines" or ordinances.

            (2) This is not true of the church of Christ. We have no authority to teach anything except that which Christ and his holy apostles taught.

CONCLUSION

1. Much more could be said of the apostle's doctrine.

2. We must believe and obey it (Romans 6:17-18).

3. We must abide in it (1 Timothy 4:16).

Some Questions About the Apostles' Doctrine

WHAT DOES THE SCRIPTURE SAY?

References: Mark 1:22; Acts 2:42; Acts 5:28; Acts 5:32; Romans 6:17-18; 1 Corinthians 4:6; 2 Corinthians 4:3-5; 2 Thessalonians 3:14; 1 Timothy 4:1; 2 Timothy 4:2-3; Galatians 1:7-9; Titus 2:10; 1 Peter 4:11; 2 John 9

1. "And they were astonished at his _____ for he taught them as one that had _____ and not as the scribes."

2. "And they continued steadfastly in the _____ _____ and fellowship, and in breaking of bread, and in prayers."

3. "Saying, Did not we straitly command you that ye should not _____ in this name? and, behold ye have filled Jerusalem with _____ _____, and intend to bring this man's blood upon us."

4. "And we are his _____ of these things; and so is also the _____ _____, whom God hath given to them that _____ him."

5. "But God be thanked, that ye were the servants of sin, but ye have _____ from the _____ that form of _____ which was delivered you. Being then made _____ from sin, ye became the _____ of righteousness."

6. "...that ye might learn in us _____ to think of _____ above that which is _____, that no one of you be puffed up for one against another."

7.   "But if our _____ be hid, it is _____ to them that are lost; In whom the god of this world hath _____ the mind of them which believe not, _____ the _____ of the glorious gospel of Christ who is the image of God, should shine unto them."

8.   "And if any _____ not our _____ by this epistle, not that man, and have no _____ with him, that he may be ashamed."

9.   "Now the Spirit speaketh expressly, that in the latter times some shall _____ from the _____, giving heed to seducing spirits, and _____ of devils."

10.   "Preach the _____; be instant in season, out of season; reprove, rebuke, exhort with all longsuffering and _____."

11.   "But though we, or an angel from heaven, _____ any other _____ unto you than that which we have _____ unto you, let him be accursed."

12.   "Not purloining, but showing all good fidelity; that they may _____ the _____ of God our Savior in all things."

13.   "If any man _____, let him speak as the _____ of God."

14.   "Whosoever transgresseth , and abideth not in the _____ of Christ hath not God. He that abideth in the _____ of Christ, he hath both the Father and the Son."

BRIEF ANSWERS

1.   What is "doctrine"? _____
_____

2.   What is "the apostles' doctrine"? _____
_____

3. Where did the apostles' doctrine originate?_____

4. Why is it important to continue in the apostles' doctrine?_____
    _____

5. Is the apostles' doctrine the same as the gospel? _____

TALK TIME—DISCUSSION

1. Discuss "doctrine" and "doctrines" as used in the New Testament.

    a. These words are used with reference to:

        (1) _____

        (2) _____

        (3) _____

        (4) _____

        (5) _____

2. Be prepared to discuss the source of the apostles' doctrine.

    a. From whom did Jesus receive his doctrine (John 7:16)? _____

    b. To whom did Jesus give the words he received of the Father
        (John 7:16)?_____

    c. When they preached that word, was it their words or the word
        of God (1 Thessalonians 2:13)? _____

    d. Why was it called "the apostles' doctrine"?_____
        _____

3. How did the apostles receive revelation of the apostles' doctrine?
    Read Galatians 1:10-11; John 14:26; 15:26; 16:13; 1 Corinthians 2:12-13.

    a. How did Paul say he received the gospel he preached? _____
        _____

    b. When the Holy Spirit came, what was he to bring to the
        memory of the apostles?_____

    c. When the Holy Spirit came to the apostles what was he to teach them? _____

    d. When did he begin this work of revelation? _____

    _____

    e. Into what did the Spirit guide them? _____

    _____

    f. Did the apostles speak the very words they received of the Spirit? _____

4.   The word "apostle" means "one sent," thus the apostles of Christ are those sent by Christ. In the outline we list four other expressions that are used of the apostles. List these four things, giving a reference for each.

    a. _____

    b. _____

    c. _____

    d. _____

5.   Discuss "witness" of Christ.

    a. What is a witness?_____

    b. What had the apostles witnessed?_____

    _____

    c. Are all Christians witnesses in this sense?_____

6.   Be prepared to discuss "ambassadors" of Christ.

    a. What is an ambassador? _____

    _____

    b. Explain how this word describes the apostles. _____

    _____

    c. Are all Christians ambassadors of Christ?_____

7.   Tell the class about the "chosen vessels" and "earthen vessels" (2 Corinthians 4:4-6; Acts 9:15).

   a.   Define "vessel" _____

   _____

   b.   Define "chosen" _____

   _____

   c.   Define "earthen" _____

   _____

   d.   What is an "earthen vessel"? _____

   _____

   e.   For what purpose were these "earthen vessels" chosen? _____

   _____

   f.   Are all Christians "earthen vessels"? _____

   g.   Are all Christians "chosen vessels" as the apostles were? _____

8.   Discuss the writing of "the apostles' doctrine."

   a.   Paul said the church at Thessalonica was taught "by word and by epistle." What is an epistle? _____

   b.   What is "scripture"? _____

   _____

   c.   What references teach that all the doctrine was written? _____

   _____

9.   List five things which tell the nature of the apostles' doctrine.

   a.   _____

   b.   _____

   c.   _____

   d.   _____

   e.   _____

10. Read Romans 6:16-18; 1 Timothy 4:16. Name three things we are to do regarding the doctrine. (Note: One of these is necessarily inferred, not mentioned specifically.)

a. _____

b. _____

c. _____

11. Tell why it is important for Christians in every generation to "continue in the apostles' doctrine."

THINK! "THINK ON THESE THINGS"

1. The apostles were men. When they taught was their teaching "the doctrines of men"? THINK! _____

2. What is the difference between "the doctrine of men" and the "apostles' doctrine"? THINK!_____
_____

3. Did the apostles have to study to know what to preach? THINK!
_____
Who took care of "what" and "how" they were to speak? THINK!
_____

4. Is there a difference between the doctrine of Christ and the doctrine of the apostles? THINK! _____

5. "Doctrine" means "teaching." Would it be the apostles' doctrine when it was written? THINK!_____
When we teach what they taught are we teaching "the apostles' doctrine"? THINK! _____

6. How can we "adorn" the doctrine of Christ? THINK! _____
_____
_____

MEMORY—"THY WORD HAVE I HID IN MINE HEART"

1. "Take heed unto thyself, and unto the doctrine; continue in them; for in doing this thou shalt both save thyself, and them that hear thee" (1 Timothy 4:16).

2. "Whosoever transgresseth, and abideth not in the doctrine of Christ, hath not God. He that abideth in the doctrine of Christ he hath both the Father and the Son" (2 John 9).

The Lord's Supper

INTRODUCTION

1. "And upon the first day of the week, when the disciples came together to break bread, Paul preached unto them" (Acts 20:7). This verse shows the practice of the early church in coming together to eat the Lord's Supper.

2. There are several terms used with reference to the Lord's Supper:

    a. Breaking of bread or break bread (Acts 2:42; 20:7)

    b. Communion (1 Corinthians 10:10)

    c. Lord's table (1 Corinthians 10:21; Cf. Luke 22:30)

    d. Lord's Supper (1 Corinthians 11:21)

3. A series of lessons on true worship would not be complete without studying the Lord's Supper.

I. What is the Lord's Supper?

    A. It is bread.

        1. "Jesus took bread, and blessed it, and brake it, and gave it to the disciples, and said, take, eat; this is my body" (Matthew 26:26).

        2. It was unleavened bread, for Jesus and the disciples were eating the feat of "the passover, and of unleavened bread" (Mark 14:1).

            a. During this feast the Jews were not permitted to have leaven in their houses.

    B. It is fruit of the vine.

        1. "And he took the cup, and gave thanks, and gave it to them, saying, Drink ye all of it...I will not drink henceforth of this fruit of the vine, until that day when I drink it new with you in my Father's kingdom" (Matthew 26:27, 29).

        2. The fruit of the vine is called "the cup." "And he took the cup, and gave thanks, and said, Take this, and divide it among yourselves: for I say unto you, I will not drink of the

fruit of the vine, until the kingdom of God shall come" (Luke 22:17-18).

    a. They divided the fruit of the vine, but Jesus took "the cup" and said "divide it among yourselves." Therefore, the cup is the fruit of the vine.

II.   The institution of the Lord's Supper

    A. Instituted by Jesus Christ

        1. The record of it (Matthew 26:26-30; Mark 14:22-26; Luke 22:17-20, 29-30)

        2. The Son of God is the founder of this Supper. Therefore, we should not consider it a small thing.

    B. Delivered to the disciples

        1. Jesus "gave it to the disciples" (Matthew 26:26).

        2. He neither expects nor demands that unbelievers eat it.

III. The place of the Lord's Supper

    A. In the kingdom of God

        1. Jesus said, "I will not drink henceforth of this fruit of the vine, until that day when I drink it new with you in my Father's kingdom" (Matthew 26:29).

        2. "And I appoint unto you a kingdom, as my Father hath appointed unto me; that ye may eat and drink at my table in my kingdom" (Luke 22:29-30).

    B. In the church

        1. The church of God at Corinth had the Lord's Supper (1 Corinthians 11:23-30).

        2. Either the church and the kingdom are the same, or they had the Lord's Supper in the wrong place.

        3. Since the apostle Paul approved of the church eating the Lord's Supper, we conclude that the church and the kingdom are the same.

IV. The time for eating the Lord's Supper

    A. "Upon the first day of the week" (Acts 20:7).

        1. The disciples had been observing the Lord's Supper since the establishment of the church (cf. Acts 2:42). This verse is the first and only reference to the day upon which

the disciples came together to break bread. There is no authority from the Lord to break the bread on any other day than "upon the first day of the week."

2. This shows that the Lord's Supper was eaten each week. Anything that is identified only by a day of the week must be a weekly occurrence. If it were monthly there would be a day of the month to designate it, if it were quarterly there would be a month and a day, and if it were annually a month and a day would be required to identify the time of observance.

3. The identical expression "upon the first day of the week" is found in 1 Corinthians 16:2, with reference to giving and everyone understands that this is weekly.

B. The time of day is not specified.

1. Each day consists of twenty-four hours. Anytime on the first day of the week would be scriptural. The practice of breaking bread at the morning worship hour is a good as anytime. Most brethren choose this hour but if some choose to break bread in the afternoon or evening they are still breaking bread on the first day of the week.

V. The purpose of the Lord's Supper

A. It is a memorial of Christ.

1. God has given memorials to his people in all ages. Examples:

a. To Noah, the bow in the clouds (Genesis 9:8-17)

b. To Israel, the Passover (Exodus 17:1-17; 23:14-18)

c. To Christians, the Lord's Supper

2. A memorial brings to mind a particular person, place or event.

a. The bow in the cloud—God's promise unto mankind

b. The Passover—the passing over the houses of the Israelites and the sparing of their firstborn

c. The Lord's Supper—Christ and his death for our sins; his body which was broken and his blood that was shed

B. To give an opportunity to teach

1. Bow in the clouds—teach God's covenant with mankind

2. Passover—Israelites could teach their children of the night God spared their firstborn

3. The Lord's Supper—gives us an opportunity to teach our children and our friends when they ask:

   a. What is this bread?

   b. Why do you drink that grape juice?

   c. Why can't I take it?

   d. What do you think about when you eat that bread and drink that grape juice?

C. It proclaims our faith in Christ.

1. When we eat the Lord's Supper we are telling the world that we believe in Christ, in his death for our sins (Matthew 26:28; 1 Corinthians 11:26).

D. It gives spiritual strength.

1. "For this cause many are weak and sickly among you, and many sleep" (1 Corinthians 11:30).

2. Instead of eating the Lord's Supper the church at Corinth was coming together for feasting. They were growing weak in spirit as a result.

VI. Some false teaching regarding the Lord's Supper

A. Closed communion

1. This is a practice among some religious groups. It is designating those who can and cannot eat.

2. The Lord teaches: "Let a man examine himself, and so let him eat of that bread, and drink of that cup" (1 Corinthians 11:28).

B. Doctrine of transubstantiation

1. This is the teaching that the bread becomes the real body of Christ, and the cup becomes the real blood of Christ. This is taught by Catholicism.

   "When our Lord said: 'This is my body' through His Almighty Power, the entire substance of the bread was changed into His body; and when he said: 'This is my blood' the entire substance of the wine was changed into His blood." (*Father Smith Instructs Jackson*, page 150).

   Concerning this change it is said: "That simply means that the color, taste, weight and shape of the bread and wine—whatever else appears to the senses remains the same after the change of the entire substance of the bread and wine into the body and blood of Christ. This change is called Transubstantiation." (Ibid. page 154)

2. Since this so-called change is not recognized by the senses, a chemical analysis would show that there has been no change.

3. The doctrine of transubstantiation has no authority to support it but the voice of Rome.

4. Jesus indeed said, "This is my body," and "this is my blood," but he was using a figure of speech, as was frequently done by inspired men.

   a. His real body was in their presence and his real blood still flowed in that body when he instituted the Lord's Supper.

C. Taking only one element—the bread

1. This is a practice of Catholicism. In explaining why the people do not take the cup, it is said:

   "If only one drop of the Precious Blood were spilled on the floor or on the clothes of the communicant, the stain would have to be removed with great care. This constitutes the practical objection against Holy Communion under both forms" (Ibid. page 160).

   "Catholics, however, who believe that the Eucharist is the living Jesus Christ, are certain that they receive not His Body alone under the form of Bread, not His Blood alone under the form of wine, but His body, Blood, Soul and Divinity under either form. The communicant, who receives, under both kinds, receives the same living Christ as he who communicates under one kind only" (*The Question Box*, page 259).

2. Jesus commanded the disciples to eat the bread and drink the cup (Matthew 26:26-28). Early Christians took both the bread and the cup (cf. 1 Corinthians 11:28; 10:16).

D. Thursday night communion

1. Many groups practice observing the Lord's Supper on Thursday night before Easter Sunday.

2. Jesus instituted the Lord's Supper on a Thursday night. But the early disciples came together on the first day of the week for breaking bread, and that with apostolic approval (Acts 20:7). Since the apostles were guided into all truth (John 16:13), we would do well to follow their approved example.

E. Monthly, quarterly or annual observance

1. Many groups practice observing the Lord's Supper monthly, bi-monthly, or quarterly. While some have no fixed number of times for observance.

2. The early disciples observed the Lord's Supper weekly (Acts 20:7).

a. "Upon the first day of the week," and each week had a "first day."

F. The one container position

1. Some brethren teach "one cup," meaning only one container. Their feelings are very strong on this point. It is made a test of fellowship. These brethren believe there can be only one container for each local church, and all must drink from this same container, or there has been no communion.

2. The cup is "the fruit of the vine" not the container. All of us believe there is one cup, i.e. the fruit of the vine.

a. Jesus took "the cup" and told the disciples to "divide it among yourselves" (Luke 22:17). It is evident that they divided the fruit of the vine and not the container.

b. "The cup of blessing which we bless, is it not the communion of the blood of Christ?" (1 Corinthians 10:16) We bless the contents, the fruit of the vine, not the container. The fruit of the vine is the communion of the blood of Christ. The container is not the communion of the blood of Christ.

c. The one cup is the fruit of the vine. Disciples all over the world bless this cup, for it is the communion of the blood of Christ.

G. The use of leavened bread

1. Some brethren are teaching that the use of unleavened bread in instituting the Lord's Supper was merely

incidental, therefore, it is not necessary to use unleavened bread. They are advocating the use of leavened bread. My first encounter of this position was in Nigeria, Africa. But it may be expected in the United States also.

2. That Jesus used unleavened bread is without dispute. Why anyone would want to practice otherwise is unknown. Where there are ingredients to make bread there would be ingredients to make unleavened bread. A departure at this point will only lead the way for other departures. We know that the use of unleavened bread is right. Why use anything else?

H. The "I'm not worthy" position

1. I have known of brethren who never eat the Lord's Supper. When asked why, they reply, "I am not worthy to take it, and if you eat when you are unworthy you eat damnation to your own soul."

2. This position is an outgrowth of misunderstanding a word. "He that eateth and drinketh **unworthily**, eateth and drinketh damnation to himself, not discerning the Lord's body" (1 Corinthians 11:29).

   a. The word "unworthily" is an adverb, describing the manner of eating. It means to eat "not discerning the Lord's body." Some at Corinth were eating a feast; they were not discerning the Lord's body but were filling their stomachs. They were eating unworthily.

   b. The word "unworthy" is an adjective. It means, "insufficient in worth; undeserving; not suiting or befitting; lacking value or merit." An adjective is used to modify a noun.

   c. In the quotation (1 Corinthians 11:29), the word "unworthily" is an adverb modifying the verbs "eateth" and "drinketh," thus describing the manner of eating and drinking.

3. Do not allow this "I'm not worthy" position keep you from obeying the Lord's command to break bread.

VII. Some abuses by brethren

A. The Sunday night communion

1. The common practice among brethren is to break bread at the Lord's Day morning worship and to have it again

that night for those who were unable to be present for the morning hour.

2. This practice has been sadly abused by those who prefer to go visiting, go fishing or picnicking, entertain friends, sleep late, work for double-time pay, and a host of other things. They miss the morning worship and come Sunday night to "take communion."

    a. While the time of day is unimportant, the practice of some is wrong. Many members think, "If I go and take the Lord's Supper I am alright."

    b. I agree with Brother Fred Dennis who wrote: "It is doubtful if the evening communion will do you any good if you missed the service when the brethren came together to break bread...Maybe if your work keeps you from the table of the Lord time after time, you had better change work!" (*Gospel Minutes*, April 30, 1965)

B. Taking the Lord's Supper to those in hospitals, etc.

    1. Some have the practice of taking the communion to all members who missed because of sickness, whether at home or in the hospital, nursing home, etc. There is even a "Minister's Communion Service" for preachers to use when carrying the communion to such persons.

    2. Such a practice may well be leading persons to think, "If I can only take communion I will be alright." What about taking the collection plate around to all who are sick or in the hospital?

    3. In the apostolic days, "the disciples came together to break bread" (Acts 20:7). There was a coming together "in one place" (1 Corinthians 11:20), for the purpose of eating the Lord's Supper. Communion is a sharing; it is a joint participation to be engaged in when the disciples come together. This would prohibit a family taking the Lord's supper with them in a picnic basket and taking time out from their recreation to "take the Lord's Supper," then go on with their fun.

    4. There may be instances when a couple or a family may have communion in their home, when they are the only disciples in an area and on the Lord's Day they worship God. But they also engage in other acts of worship. There

may be other situations where this would be acceptable. However, the rule is: "The disciples came together to break bread."

C. Making the Lord's Supper a mere rite or ceremony

1. We must eat discerning the Lord's body and blood, or else we eat and drink damnation to ourselves. See 1 Corinthians 11:29.

2. In eating the Lord's Supper let us be sure we remember the Lord, his body and his blood. Let us not eat and drink just out of habit. Do not just go through a form.

CONCLUSION

1. The Lord's Supper is a memorial, instituted by our Lord, to be observed by all his disciples upon the first day of the week in memory of him.

2. We have enjoyed and continue to enjoy the benefits of his death for us, so let us observe the Lord's Supper in grateful appreciation for that sacrifice for our sins. Let us not forget this friend of friends.

Some Questions About the Lord's Supper

WHAT DOES THE SCRIPTURE SAY?

References: Matthew 26:26-30; Mark 14:22-26; Luke 22:17-20; Luke 22:29-30; Acts 2:42; Acts 20:7; 1 Corinthians 10:16-20; 1 Corinthians 11:17-34.

1. "And as they were eating, Jesus took _____, and blessed it, and _____ it, and gave it to the disciples, and said, Take _____ this is my _____."

2. "And he took the _____, and gave thanks, and gave it to them, saying, _____ ye _____ of it; for this is my _____ which is shed for many _____ the remission of sins."

3. "Verily I say unto you, I will _____ no more of the _____ of the _____, until that day that I drink it new in the _____ of God."

4. "And he took the _____ and gave thanks, and said, Take this, and _____ it among yourselves."

5. "This cup is the _____ _____ my blood, which is shed for you."

6. "And I appoint unto you a _____, as my Father hath appointed unto me; that ye may _____ and _____ at my table in my _____."

7. "And they continued steadfastly in the apostles' doctrine and in fellowship and in _____ of _____, and in prayers."

8. "And upon the _____ day of the _____, when the disciples came together to _____, Paul preached unto them."

9. "The _____ of blessing which we bless, is it not the _____ of the _____ of Christ?"

10. "The bread which we _____, is it not the _____ of the body of Christ?"

11. "Ye can not drink the _____ of the Lord, and the cup of _____; ye cannot be partakers of the _____ table and of the table of devils."

12. "When ye come together therefore in one place, this is not to eat the _____ _____. For in eating every one taketh before other his own _____ and one is hungry, and another is drunken."

13. "What? have ye not _____ to eat and to drink in? or despise ye the church of _____, and shame them that have not? what shall I say to you? shall I praise you in this? I _____ you not."

14. "For I have received of the Lord that which also I delivered unto you, that the _____ Jesus the same night in which he was betrayed took _____: and when he had given thanks, he brake it, and said, _____ eat: this is my _____, which is broken for you: this do in _____ of me."

15. "After the same manner also he took the _____, when he had supped, saying, this cup is the _____ testament in my blood: this do ye, as oft as ye _____ it, in _____ of me."

16. "For as _____ as ye eat this _____, and drink this _____, ye do show the Lord's death till he come."

17. "Wherefore whosoever shall eat this bread, and drink this cup of the Lord, _____, shall be guilty of the body and the blood of the _____."

18. "But let a man _____ himself, and so let him eat of that bread, and drink of that cup."

19. "For he that eateth and drinketh _____, eateth and drinketh _____ to himself, not _____ the Lord's body."

20. "And if any man hunger, let him _____ at home; that ye come not together unto condemnation."

TALK TIME—DISCUSSION

1. What are the terms used in the scripture with reference to the Lord's Supper? Give a reference for each.

    a. _____

    b. _____

    c. _____

    d. _____

2. The Lord's Supper consists of two elements, what are they? _____
    _____

3. What kind of bread was used? _____
    How do you know? _____
    _____

4. What is the cup? _____

5. By whose authority is the Lord's Supper eaten? _____
    _____

6. Where did the Lord place the Lord's table? Give the reference.
    _____

7.   When did the early disciples break bread? _____
_____

8.   Be prepared to discuss the Lord's Supper as a memorial, and some
other memorials God has given.

   a.   What is the purpose of a memorial? _____
_____

   b.   Name some other memorials God has given. _____
_____

   c.   What was the purpose of those memorials? _____
_____

   d.   How is the Lord's Supper a memorial? _____
_____

9.   Memorials give people an opportunity to teach. After each of the
following memorials tell what can be taught.

   a.   Bow in the clouds._____
_____

   b.   The passover. _____
_____

   c.   The Lord's Supper. _____
_____

10.   What does our eating the Lord's Supper proclaim unto the world?
_____

11.   In your own words tell what you think of when you:

   a.   Break the bread. _____
_____

   b.   Drink the cup. _____
_____

12.   How were those at Corinth perverting the Lord's Supper? _____
_____

a.   Did they really eat the Lord's Supper? _____

13.   Explain the difference between "unworthily" and "unworthy."

_____

14.   What does it mean to discern the Lord's body?_____

_____

15.   Who is to examine the people and determine who should eat and who should not?_____

16.   The cup is the "communion of the blood of Christ" and the bread is the "communion of the body of Christ." What does this mean?

_____

17.   There are several false doctrines relating to the Lord's Supper. List these and be prepared to show why each is wrong.

a.   _____

b.   _____

c.   _____

d.   _____

e.   _____

f.   _____

g.   _____

h.   _____

18.   The saints at Corinth abused the Lord's Supper by turning it into a feast. Tell how some brethren abuse it today._____

_____

_____

19.   Should the local church have the practice of taking the Lord's Supper to all the members who cannot or do not come together to break bread? _____ Explain your answer. _____

_____

20.   How can we avoid making the Lord's Supper a mere ceremony?

_____

_____

    THINK! "THINK ON THESE THINGS"

1.   How does the fact that the Lord's table was in the church at Corinth with apostolic approval, show that the church and the kingdom are the same? THINK! _____

_____

2.   What is the difference between "the doctrine of men" and the "apostles' doctrine"? THINK!_____

_____

3.   When Jesus took the cup and gave it to his disciples, he said, "Divide it among yourselves." What did they divide? THINK! _____ Is this the same as Mark's statement, "and they all drank of it"? (Mark 14:23) THINK! _____ Does this statement teach there is but one container? THINK! _____

4.   Paul said, "For we are all partakers of that one bread" (see 1 Corinthians 10:17). Does this mean we all break from the same piece of bread? THINK! _____ Does it mean we all partake of one kind of bread, i.e., unleavened bread? THINK! _____ Paul was in Ephesus when he wrote the 1 Corinthians letter (see 1 Corinthians 16:8, 9). Yet, he and the saints at Corinth were partakers of that one bread. Could they have eaten the same piece of bread? THINK! _____ Could they partake of the same kind of bread? THINK! _____

5.   The Lord's Supper was given to the disciples. Does this mean it is sinful for non-members to eat? THINK! _____ Are they any more lost after eating? THINK! _____ Should we practice closed communion? THINK! _____

6.   What was the spiritual condition of some at Corinth when they
      failed to eat the Lord's Supper? THINK! _____
      If we fail to eat will we become as they were? THINK! _____

7.   Jesus instituted the Lord's Supper on a Thursday night. Does this
      authorize our eating it on Thursday night? THINK! _____ If not,
      why not? _____

      _____

8.   Paul said, "As often as ye eat this bread, and drink this cup, ye do
      show the Lord's death till he come." They why not do it every day—
      that would be "often"? THINK! _____

      _____

9.   We are not to eat and drink "unworthily." If we know we have
      sinned during the week should we partake of the Lord's Supper?
      THINK! _____

10.   Does our having committed a sin have anything to do with eating
      unworthily? THINK! _____

11.   The Lord's Supper is communion, sharing or joint participation.
      Can we forsake the assembling of the saints and take the supper
      off by ourself? THINK! _____

MEMORY—"THY WORD HAVE I HID IN MINE HEART"

1.   "Jesus took bread, and blessed it, and brake it, and gave it to the
      disciples, and said, Take, eat; this is my body. And he took the cup,
      and gave thanks, and gave it to them, saying, Drink ye all of it; for
      this is my blood of the New Testament, which is shed for many for
      the remission of sins" (Matthew 26:26-28).

2.   "And upon the first day of the week, when the disciples came
      together to break bread, Paul preached unto them" (Acts 20:7).

A Study of Fellowship

INTRODUCTION

1. Of those three thousand who were baptized into Christ on Pentecost day (Acts 2) it is said, "And they continued steadfastly in the apostles' doctrine and fellowship, and in breaking of bread and in prayers" (vs. 42).

2. The word "fellowship" is used in several ways in the New Testament. We propose to study its usage in this lesson that we may learn the significance of fellowship, what scriptural fellowship involves and how fellowship is obtained and continued.

3. Before studying fellowship it will be in order to define the word:

   a. Thayer's *Greek-English Lexicon of the New Testament* gives three definitions of the Greek word *koinonia* which is translated "fellowship." He says: "1. the share which one has in anything, participation. 2. intercourse, fellowship, intimacy. 3. a benefaction jointly contributed, a collection, a contribution."

   b. W. E. Vine defines it: "(a) communion, fellowship, sharing in common, (b) that which is the outcome of fellowship, a contribution" (*An Expository Dictionary of New Testament Words*).

I. The usage of the word "fellowship" in the New Testament

A. The word fellowship is found fifteen times in the New Testament.

   1. Twelve of these times it comes from the word *koinonia* which we defined above.

      a. "in worship they continued...in fellowship" (Acts 2:42)

      b. "call unto the fellowship of his Son" (1 Corinthians 1:9)

      c. "The fellowship of ministering to the saints" (2 Corinthians 8:4)

      d. "the right hands of fellowship" (Galatians 2:9)

      e. "What is the fellowship of the mystery?" (Ephesians 3:9)

      f. "For your fellowship in the gospel" (Philippians 1:5)

g. "if any fellowship of the spirit" (Philippians 2:1)

h. "the fellowship of his sufferings" (Philippians 3:10)

i. "that ye may have fellowship with us" (1 John 1:3)

j. "Our fellowship is with the Father, and with his Son Jesus Christ" (1 John 1:3)

k. "If we say that we have fellowship" (1 John 1:6)

l. "we have fellowship one with another" (1 John 1:7)

Note: This same word *koinonia* is translated:

a. "Communion" (four times)

    (1) communion of the blood (1 Corinthians 10:16)

    (2) communion of the body (1 Corinthians 10:16)

    (3) What communion hath light with (2 Corinthians 6:14)

    (4) the communion of the Holy Ghost (2 Corinthians 13:14)

b. "Contribution" (one time)

    (1) Macedonia and Achaia made a contribution for the saints at Jerusalem (Romans 15:26).

c. "Distribution" (one time)

    (1) "for your liberal distribution" (2 Corinthians 9:13)

d. "Communication" (one time)

    (1) "that the communication of thy..." (Philemon 6)

e. "To communicate" (one time)

    (1) "willing to communicate" (1 Timothy 6:18)

2. One time from *koinonos*, "to become a partaker"

a. "I would not that ye should have fellowship with devils" (1 Corinthians 10:20).

3. One time from *sunkoinoneo*, "to have fellowship with, be a partner with"

a. "Have no fellowship with the unfruitful works of darkness" (Ephesians 5:11).

4. One time from *netoche*, meaning "partnership"

a. "What fellowship hath righteousness with unrighteousness?" (2 Corinthians 6:14)

    B. The word fellowship is found but one time in the Old Testament.

        1. From the Hebrew word *chabar*, meaning "to be joined." "Shall the throne of iniquity have fellowship with thee, which frameth mischief by law?" (Psalm 94:20)

II. Things to observe from the usage of "fellowship" in the New Testament

    A. A Christian can have fellowship:

        1. With God (1 John 1:3, 6, 7)

            a. How? By being born again (John 3:5), thus all of the same Father (Galatians 3:26) and partakers of his divine nature (2 Peter 1:4)

        2. With Christ (1 Corinthians 1:9; 1 John 1:3)

            a. How?

                (1) We are of the same Father (Hebrews 2:9).

                (2) By abiding in his doctrine (2 John 9)

        3. With the Spirit (Philippians 2:1; 2 Corinthians 13:14)

            a. How?

                (1) We are led by the Spirit (Romans 8:14).

                (2) The Spirit dwells in us (Romans 8:9; Galatians 4:4, 5).

        4. With one another (Galatians 2:9; 1 John 1:7)

            a. How?

                (1) By walking in the light (1 John 1:7)

                    (a) The gospel is the light (2 Corinthians 4:4); the word of God is the light (Psalm 119:105, 130).

                (2) When a disciple transgresses the doctrine of Christ, he is no longer walking in the light (2 John 9).

        5. In worship (Acts 2:42)

            a. How?

                (1) We are joint participants in the worship unto God (John 4:24; Ephesians 5:19).

        6. In ministering to the saints (2 Corinthians 8:4)

            a. How?

        (1) By making gifts of contributions to their needs (Romans 15:26). Macedonia and Achaia made a certain "contribution" to the saints (2 Corinthians 9:13). Paul calls it their "liberal distribution unto them."

7. In the gospel (Philippians 1:5)

    a. How?

        (1) By teaching the gospel and supporting the gospel preachers (Philippians 1:3-5; 2:22; 4:15-17)

8. In His sufferings (Philippians 3:10)

    a. How?

        (1) By suffering with him (Romans 8:17; 2 Timothy 2:12)

Note: The fellowship we have with God, with Christ, with the Spirit, with one another—in worship, in ministering to the saints, in the gospel, in his sufferings—pertains to things spiritual. There is nothing in the New Testament to cause one to conclude that the fellowship of Christians includes eating and drinking together, providing recreation and entertainment. Fifty years ago, J. D. Tant and others were warning brethren of dangers along this line, when they said, "Brethren, we are drifting."

B. A Christian must not have fellowship:

1. With devils (1 Corinthians 10:20)

Note: We have participation with Christ in Christian worship at the Lord's table in his kingdom in observance of the Lord's Supper (1 Corinthians 10:16-21).

    a. In Jewish worship the altar where God's name was recorded represented the presence of God to the Jews.

        (1) Those who ate of the Jewish sacrifices became "partakers" of the altar (v. 18) which meant to them "participation with God."

    b. In like manner in the assembly of the saints, when the bread and the cup are taken in commemoration of his death, there is "communion" (fellowship) with Christ, with His body and His blood, and there is participation or sharing with Christ, personally (v. 16).

    c. In such observance of the Lord's Supper, there is common union (fellowship) with Christ upon the part of Christians and therefore common union (fellowship) with each other in this worship.

   d. Just as union with Christ and with one another in the Lord's Supper is true (exists), so also participation affords and expresses union and fellowship with Christ in fellowship with another in the body of Christ (v. 17).

   e. The argument concludes with the fact that those who participate in this false worship serve Satan rather than God and as a result cannot be identified with or participate with Christ (v. 21).

Note: Surely this plain teaching condemns those who think they can fellowship religious error, participate in it and encourage it, or bid God's speed to those who take part in its practice and promotion and still have "fellowship" with Christ.

"Ye cannot be partakers of the Lord's table and of the table of devils."

2. With "the works of darkness" (Ephesians 5:11)

   a. The "works of darkness" are set forth in the context (verses 1-8).

     (1) We are to withdraw from those who walk disorderly (2 Thessalonians 3:6, 10-14).

     (2) "With such an one no not to eat" (1 Corinthians 5:9-11).

   b. Christians have been called out of the darkness of the world and are not to maintain fellowship with the works of darkness (Acts 26:18; Romans 12:1-2).

   c. "If we say that we have fellowship with him, and walk in darkness, we lie, and do not the truth" (1 John 1:6).

C. There is no fellowship of righteousness with unrighteousness.

1. Righteousness has to do with that which is right, just, upright, i.e., with the will of God for us.

2. "Unrighteousness" means "lawlessness." In this text the word is from the Greek *anomia*, which is found 14 times in the New Testament:

   a. Twelve times it is translated "iniquity." Matthew 7:23; 13:41; 2 Thessalonians 2:7; Hebrews 8:12, 10:17.

        b. One time it is translated "transgression of the law" ("for sin is the transgression of the law," 1 John 3:4).

        c. One time it is translated "unrighteousness" (2 Corinthians 6:14).

3. Christians must have no fellowship with those who practice "unrighteousness" (lawlessness) or who work iniquity.

        a. Missionary Societies and mechanical instruments of music in worship were works of iniquity (lawlessness), and our fathers did not maintain fellowship with those who introduced such into the church of our Lord.

        b. We are to "mark them which cause divisions and offences contrary to the doctrine of Christ" (Romans 16:17).

        c. Those who transgress the doctrine of Christ do not have God or Christ (2 John 9-11). Why should we want to fellowship them?

CONCLUSION

1.   When one believes and obeys the gospel of Christ he is brought into fellowship with God and Christ and with all others who have obeyed the gospel.

2.   "If we walk in the light, as he is in the light" (1 John 1:7), we continue in fellowship with both the Father and the Son and with all others who are walking in the light.

3.   "Don't worry about fellowship. Just preach the gospel and get people to walk in the light and the fellowship will take care of itself. We have 'full fellowship' when we thus walk."—Fred E. Dennis (*Truth Magazine*, Vol. X, No. 10, July 1966)

4.   "If we still all preach the gospel without fear or favor, if we will speak boldly and plainly, if we will expose error within and without the church, the question and the matter of fellowship will take care of itself. Those who love the truth will be one mind in it. Those who don't love the truth will go out from us as they have always done. If the truth of God won't hold them, all the ideas for a false unity that...brethren can concoct will do absolutely no good."—Bill Cavender (*Truth Magazine*, Vol. XIV, No. 5, Dec. 4, 1969)

5.   Thank God that we can have fellowship with him and with all others who faithfully serve him.

We Have Fellowship

1. With God — How? — **Born again**
1 John 1:3   John 3:5

2. With Christ — How? — **Of same Father**
1 Corinthians 1:9   Hebrews 2:9

3. With Spirit — How? — **He dwells in us**
Philippians 2:1   Romans 8:9, 16; Galatians 4:4-5

4. With one another — How? — **Walk in the light**
Galatians 2:9   1 John 1:7

5. In worship — How? — **Joint participants**
Acts 2:42   John 4:24; Ephesians 5:19

6. In ministering to saints — How? — **Contribution:** Romans 15:26
2 Corinthians 8:4   **Distribution:** 2 Corinthians 9:13

7. In the gospel — How? — **Supporting preachers**
Philippians 1:3-5   Philippians 4:15-18

8. In His sufferings — How? — **Suffering with Him**
Philippians 3:10   1 Peter 4:13; Romans 8:17

No Fellowship

1. With devils: 1 Corinthians 10:20

2. With works of darkness: Ephesians 5:11

Some Questions About Fellowship

 WHAT DOES THE SCRIPTURE SAY?

References: Acts 2:42; 1 Corinthians 1:9; 2 Corinthians 8:4; Galatians 2:9; Ephesians 3:9; Philippians 1:5; Philippians 2:1; Philippians 3:10; 1 John 1:3; 1 John 1:6; 1 John 1:7; 1 Corinthians 10:20; Ephesians 5:11; 2 Corinthians 6:14

1. "And they continued steadfastly in the apostles' doctrine and _____, and in breaking of _____ and in _____."

2. "God is _____, by whom ye were called unto the _____ of his son Jesus Christ our Lord."

3. "Praying us with much _____ that we would receive the gift, and take upon us the _____ of the _____ to the saints."

4. "...They gave to me and Barnabas the _____ _____ of _____; that we should go unto the heathen, and they unto the _____."

5. "And to make all men see what is the _____ of the _____, which from the beginning of the world hath been hid in _____, who created all things by Jesus Christ."

6. "For your _____ in the _____ from the first day until now."

7. "If there be therefore, any _____ in Christ, if any comfort of love, if any _____ of the _____, if any bowels and mercies."

8. "That I may know him, and the power of his _____ and the _____ of his _____ being made conformable unto his death."

9. "That which we have seen and heard declare we unto you, that ye also may have _____ with us: and truly our _____ is with the _____, and with his Son Jesus Christ."

10. "If we say that we have _____ with him, and walk in _____, we lie, and do not the _____."

11. "But if we walk in the _____, as he is in the _____ we have _____ one with another, and the blood of Jesus Christ his Son cleanseth us from all sin."

12. "But I say, that the things which the Gentiles sacrifice, they sacrifice to _____, and not to _____: and I would not that ye should have _____ with _____."

13. "And have no _____ with the _____ works of _____, but rather reprove them."

14. "Be ye not unequally yoked together with _____ for what _____ hath _____ with _____? And what communion hath light and darkness?"

BRIEF ANSWERS

1. What are the three definitions of the Greek word "Koinonia" which is translated fellowship, as given by Thayer? _____

    _____

    _____

2. How does W. E. Vine define fellowship? _____

    _____

3. How many times is the word "fellowship" found in the New Testament?_____

4. How many times is the word "fellowship" found in the Old Testament?_____

5. Does the word of God restrict the bounds of our fellowship? _____

TALK TIME—DISCUSSION

1. The Greek word *koinonia* that is translated into the English word "fellowship" is also translated into four other English words. What are they and where are they found in the New Testament?

    a. _____

    b. _____

    c. _____

    d. _____

2. The Christian is in fellowship with God.

    a. Give a reference which shows we are in fellowship with God.
        _____

    b. How did we get into His fellowship? _____
        _____

3. Each disciple of Christ has fellowship with Christ.

    a. Why do we have such fellowship? _____
        _____

    b. How do we continue in his fellowship? _____
        _____

4. Discuss our fellowship with the Spirit.

    a. Cite a reference which shows we have fellowship with the Spirit._____

    b. How did we come into this fellowship? _____
        _____

    c. How do we continue in this fellowship? _____
        _____

5. Christians have fellowship with one another.

    a.   Tell how we came into fellowship with one another. _____

    _____

    b.   How do we continue in fellowship with each other?_____

    _____

6.   There are certain acts in which Christians become partners or sharers. In these acts we have fellowship. What are they? _____

    _____

    _____

7.   How do Christians have fellowship in worship? _____

    _____

8.   The Corinthians entreated Paul that they might share in the "fellowship of the ministering to the saints" (2 Corinthians 8:4). Tell how this fellowship is accomplished. _____

    _____

    _____

9.   How can we have fellowship in the gospel? _____

    _____

10.   Can Christians have fellowship in the sufferings of Christ? If so, how?_____

    _____

11.   What is "the fellowship of the mystery" (Ephesians 3:9)? _____

    _____

12.   Name two things with which Christians are NOT to have fellowship.

    _____

    _____

13.   What is meant by "the cup of devils" and "the table of devils" in 1 Corinthians 10:21? _____

    _____

14.   After reading 2 Corinthians 6:16 be prepared to discuss righteousness and unrighteousness.

a. What fellowship is there of righteousness with unrighteousness? _____

b. The word translated "unrighteousness" is the Greek word *anomia*. Into what English word is *anomia* usually translated?

_____

c. What will happen to the "workers of iniquity" at the judgment?

_____

d. Should the Christian continue in fellowship with those who work "unrighteousness" (lawlessness)? _____

15. What course of action is to be taken toward them who walk "contrary to the doctrine of Christ?"_____

_____

THINK! "THINK ON THESE THINGS"

1. Fellowship is the same as communion (common union). When we eat the Lord's Supper in what do we have communion? THINK!

_____

2. As Christians we enjoy "fellowship with the Father, and with his Son Jesus Christ" (1 John 1:3). When a Christian transgresses the doctrine of Christ, what happens to that fellowship he had with the Father and the Son? THINK! _____

_____

3. Should we continue to give "the right hands of fellowship" (Cf. Galatians 2:9) to those who have transgressed the doctrine of Christ? THINK!_____

4. We are commanded to "walk as children of light" and "have no fellowship with the unfruitful works of darkness" (Ephesians 5:8, 11). If a brother or sister persists in walking in darkness should we continue in fellowship with him? THINK! _____

5.   If we say we have fellowship with God, and walk in darkness, what have we become? (1 John 1:6) THINK!_____

6.   Should we want to fellowship one in that condition? THINK! _____

7.   Read the statement by brother Fred E. Dennis (See conclusion of outline, point 3.) Do you agree with this statement? THINK!_____

8.   In view of the scriptures studied in this lesson, do you think we should extend the "right hands of fellowship" to those who have never been baptized into Christ? THINK! _____

9.   From the chart on fellowship, in the preceding lesson, observe that Christians have fellowship with other persons. Who are those persons? THINK!_____

_____

10.   From that same chart we observe that Christians have become partners of have fellowship in certain acts. What are those acts? THINK!_____

_____

11.   Does the fellowship of Christians involve entertainment and or recreation? THINK! _____

 MEMORY—"THY WORD HAVE I HID IN MINE HEART"

1.   "That which we have seen and heard declare we unto you, that ye also may have fellowship with us: and truly our fellowship is with the Father, and with his Son Jesus Christ" (1 John 1:3).

2.   "If we say that we have fellowship with him, and walk in darkness, we lie, and do not the truth" (1 John 1:6).

3.   "Whosoever transgresseth , and abideth not in the doctrine of Christ, hath not God. He that abideth in the doctrine of Christ he hath both the Father and the Son" (2 John 9).

Fellowship in Giving

INTRODUCTION

1.   Giving of our means is an act of spiritual worship and service, and when we contribute on the Lord's day into the common treasury of the Lord's church, we are having fellowship in spiritual matters.

2.   In this series of lessons on worship, the word "fellowship" (Acts 2:42) has reference to the act of sharing things in common, or the giving that supplied the needs of the saints.

3.   In His wisdom our Lord knew that we would have problems with our giving, so he taught more on giving than on the Lord's Supper and baptism combined. It is said that in the New Testament "one verse out of every five deals with money." The will of the Lord was summed up in one statement, "...remember the words of the Lord Jesus, how he said, It is more blessed to give than to receive" (Acts 20:35).

4.   Each Christian must be taught the will of the Lord on giving, so he may "abound in this grace also" (2 Corinthians 8:7).

I.   The individual in God's plan for giving

    A.   Giving is a personal matter (1 Corinthians 16:1-2).

        1.   "Let every one of you lay by him in store..."

            a.   We should teach our children the principle of giving.

> Ah, when I look up at the cross
> Where God's great steward suffered loss
> Yea, loss of life and blood for me?
> A trifling thing it seems to be
> To give liberally Lord, to thee.
> Of time or talents, wealth or store
> Full well I know I owe thee more
> A million times I owe thee more.
> —V. P. Black, *Rust as a Witness*, p. 13

    B.   Individual enterprise makes giving possible.

        1.   God's plan calls for every man to work to support himself and those who depend upon him, and to have to give to

others and to the Lord (1 Thessalonians 4:11-12; 2 Thessalonians 3:10; Ephesians 4:28).

2. The Lord's church is not to engage in business for the purpose of supporting the work it is assigned to do but is to be supported by the free will offerings of the members. This is the Lord's plan.

II. The motive in giving

A. A divine command.

1. Jesus said: "Give to him that asketh thee, and from him that would borrow of thee, turn not thou away" (Matthew 5:42).

2. "Give and it shall be given unto you; good measure, pressed down, and shaken together, and running over..."

3. Each Christian is commanded to "lay by him in store" (1 Corinthians 16:1-2).

B. It makes us God-like to give.

1. To learn how God has given should help us in our giving. He has given:

a. Sacrificially (John 3:16)

b. Freely (Romans 8:32)

c. Liberally (James 1:5)

d. Everything that we have (Acts 17:25; James 1:17)

2. Each of us should try to imitate this divine nature of giving.

Thank God for the blessings He's given
And share of the good you've in store;
Remember, though great your endeavor,
Your Savior has given much more.
—V. P. Black, Ibid., p. 19

C. It opens the doorway into the bounty of God's grace.

1. We reap as we sow (Galatians 6:6-10; 2 Corinthians 9:6).

2. Give and it shall be given unto you (Luke 6:38).

a. We can never out-give the Lord.

"A man who was noted for his liberal giving was asked how he could afford to give so much. He replied, "When I was poor and did not have much to give, I started shoveling out and God started shoveling in and God used a bigger shovel than I did." This has always been God's promise to his people. No one can outgive God" (Ibid., p. 65).

D. It is the way to be happy.

　　1. "It is more blessed to give than to receive" (Acts 20:35). O, the joy of giving.

　　2. Never discourage anyone from giving. When you do you rob them of the joy of giving. Consider the widow and her "two mites" (Mark 12:41-44).

E. It is a means of glorifying God.

　　1. Each Christian is to glorify Him (1 Corinthians 6:20; 10:31).

　　2. My giving serves to glorify him (2 Corinthians 9:12-15; Cf. Matthew 10:42).

F. It is a means of laying up treasures in heaven (Matthew 6:19-20; 1 Timothy 6:17-19).

　　1. The greater my treasure in heaven, the greater my desire to go there.

　　2. The story is told of a man who was made "king of an island" for one day. He did not relax and demand that the others wait on him. But he had all his subjects working, that day, transferring goods to another island which belonged to him. After his day as king had ended he then moved to the island where all the good had been transferred. We have a lifetime to lay up for ourselves treasures in heaven. What are we doing about it?

　　　　"Everything that God made will follow its treasure. It is impossible for a man to be very interested in heaven without having treasure there. Brother or sister, are you laying up treasures in heaven?" (Ibid. p. 25)

G. It lends acceptance to our prayers.

　　1. "The eyes of the Lord are over the righteous, and his ears are open unto their prayers" (1 Peter 3:12).

III. How should I give?

A. The New Testament plan for giving (1 Corinthians 16:1-2; 2 Corinthians 9:6-8).

　　1. Regularly—"Upon the first day of the week."

2. Personally—"let every one of them."

3. Proportionately—"as God has prospered him."

4. Preventively—"That there be no gatherings..."

5. Voluntarily—"not grudgingly nor of necessity."

    a. What would you think of a man who brought his wife a gift and threw it at her saying, "I didn't really want to buy it, but I knew you would expect it"?

6. Purposely—"as he purposeth in his heart."

    a. God does not want the "left overs", so plan and purpose your giving.

7. Confidently—"God is able to make all grace abound toward you..." (2 Corinthians 9:8; Matthew 6:33, 34)

8. Cheerfully—"God loves a cheerful giver."

B. What about tithing? How much should I give?

1. What about tithing? Often members of the church say, "We are not under the law, so we do not have to give a tenth."

    a. It is true that we are not under the law, for it ended at the cross (Cf. Ephesians 2:12-16; Colossians 2:14).

    b. Tithing did not begin with the law of Moses.

        (1) Abraham paid tithes to Melchizedek four hundred years before the law (Genesis 14:19-20).

        (2) Jacob vowed to give a tenth unto God (Genesis 28:20-22).

    c. There must have been some teaching on tithing before the days of Abraham, therefore before the law.

    d. Someone says, "There is no record of it."

        (1) There is no record of teaching on murder before Cain slew Abel, but Cain was punished for it.

        (2) There is no record of breaking bread on the first day of the week until Acts 20:7, but this does not mean they were breaking bread on some other day.

    e. The Law of Moses commanded tithing (Numbers 18:20-24; Deuteronomy 12; 14:22).

        (1) When they failed to give a tithe they were said to be robbing God (Cf. Malachi 3:8).

"If it had been left to every man to give for religious purposes as he pleased—how should so many people have hit upon a tenth for God's portion rather than a fifth, or a fifteenth, etc. Does not the universality of this proportion point to a time when the ancestors of those nation lived together, and so derived the custom from a common source?" (Ibid. p. 41)

"Brethren, we had better wake up, for many have the wrong attitude toward money. Remember this, we never read of any people in any age of the world who ever gave less than a tenth of their income to God, and at the same time met the approval of God" (Ibid. p. 17).

2. The New Testament teaches liberality.

   a. The first converts were Jews who had been giving a tenth, plus many free will offerings. Would they now give less after being saved?

   b. God wants us to give liberally and bountifully because we want to give, not out of a feeling of necessity (Cf. 2 Corinthians 9:6-7).

   c. Remember: the Old Testament was written "for our learning" (Romans 15:4). From it we learn how God wanted men to give. Have we truly learned this lesson on giving?

   "When we study the Old Testament and learn how those people were required to give, it should make most of us feel so ashamed of the little we give" (Ibid. p. 12).

3. Each disciple is to give "as God hath prospered him" (1 Corinthians 16:2).

   a. Our giving "is accepted according to that a man hath" (2 Corinthians 8:12).

   b. If each gives "as God hath prospered him" there will be equality in the grace of giving.

   "Someone has said if you get all you can and save all you can and do not give all you can, then you are twofold more the child of hell than you were before."

"Someone has said givers are like wells: there is the well from which you have to draw the water. Some wells have to be pumped. Some wells are over-flowing with water. What kind are you? Will you help restore New Testament giving?" (Ibid. p.49)

CONCLUSION

1.   Let us thank God for the prosperity he has given us and cheerfully give according to that prosperity. No doubt many people of God will be lost because of covetousness. We must love God more than we love money, and strive for treasures in heaven more than for treasures on earth. Let us be more concerned with eternal security than with social security.

Some Questions About Giving

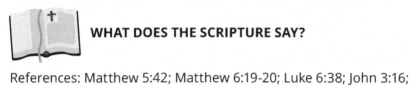

WHAT DOES THE SCRIPTURE SAY?

References: Matthew 5:42; Matthew 6:19-20; Luke 6:38; John 3:16;
Acts 17:25; Acts 20:35; 1 Corinthians 16:2; 2 Corinthians 8:7;
2 Corinthians 9:6; Galatians 6:6; 1 Thessalonians 4:11; 1 Timothy 6:16-17;
Hebrews 7:4; Genesis 28:20-22; Malachi 3:8; Romans 15:4

1. "_____ to him that _____ thee, and from him that
   would _____ of thee turn not thou away."

2. "Lay not up for yourselves _____ upon _____ where
   moth and rust doth _____, and where _____ break
   through and steal: But lay up for yourselves _____ in
   _____..."

3. "_____ and it shall be _____ unto you; good measure,
   pressed down, and shaken together, and running over, shall men
   _____ into your bosom. For with the same _____ that
   ye mete withal it shall be _____ to you again."

4. "For _____ so loved the _____, that he gave his only
   begotten _____, that whosoever _____ on him should
   not _____ but have everlasting life."

5. "Neither is _____ with men's _____ as though he
   needed anything, seeing he _____ to all life, and breath, and
   _____ _____."

6. "I have showed you all things, how that so _____ ye ought
   to _____ the weak, and remember the words of the Lord
   Jesus, how he said, It is more blessed to _____ than to
   _____."

7. "Upon the _____ day of the _____ let every one of you _____ by him in store, as God hath _____ him, that there be no _____ when I come."

8. "Therefore, as ye _____ in every thing, in _____ and utterance, and _____, and in all diligence and in your _____ to us, see that ye abound in this _____ also."

9. "But this I say, He which soweth _____ shall reap _____; and he which soweth _____ shall reap also _____."

10. "Let him that is taught in the word _____ unto him that _____ in all good things."

11. "And that ye _____ to be _____, and to do your own _____, and to work with your own hands, as we _____ you."

12. "_____ up in store for themselves a good _____ against the _____ to come, that they may lay hold on _____ life."

13. "And Jacob _____ a vow, saying...of all that thou shalt give _____ I will surely _____ the _____ unto thee."

14. "Will a man _____ God? Yet ye have _____ me. But ye say, Wherein have we _____ thee? In _____ and offerings."

15. "For whatsoever things were written _____ were written for our _____, that we through patience and _____ of the Scriptures might have _____."

TALK TIME—DISCUSSION

1. Give two examples from the O.T. which show that the people of God have always been taught to give. _____

_____

_____

2. When the law was given to Israel how much were they commanded to give? _____

3. When the church was established (Acts 2) were the members taught to give? (See Acts 2:42-45.) _____

4. How should the church of today raise the money to carry on its work?_____
    _____

5. People must be motivated to give. What are the motives for our giving?

    a. _____

    b. _____

    c. _____

    d. _____

    e. _____

    f. _____

    g. _____

6. What did Jesus mean? "Give to him that asketh thee" (Matthew 5:42).
    _____
    _____

7. Tell how giving makes us God-like. _____
    _____

8. What are the characteristics of God's giving to us?_____
    _____
    _____

9. Explain what "sowing and reaping" has to do with giving (Galatians 6:6-8). _____
    _____

10. Do you believe you can out-give the Lord? _____

11. How can giving help one to be happy? _____
_____
_____

12. Does our giving glorify God? _____
How? _____
_____

13. Tell how we can lay up for ourselves treasures in heaven. _____
_____
_____

14. Tell how one an explained his ability to give so liberally. _____
_____
_____

15. In your own words tell how we should give. _____
_____
_____

ABOUT TITHING

1. What is a tithe? _____
_____

2. Was tithing commanded under the law of Moses? _____

3. Was tithing practiced before the law? _____
Name some who tithed. _____
_____

4. Did they give in addition to the tithe? _____

5. When Jacob vowed to give a tenth unto the Lord did he have it at
that moment? _____
Was he vowing to give a tenth of all God gave him? _____

6. When people tithe do they give this as God has prospered them?
_____

7. Did the Jews have as great blessings under the law as they had when they obeyed the gospel? _____

8. Since the Jews were giving a tenth before they became Christians, do you think they would begin giving less after they became Christians? _____

9. Are we taught to purpose how much we will give? _____

10. Are Christians commanded to give a tenth? _____

11. Can you read in the Scriptures of any one who gave less than a tenth to God and at the same time met the approval of God?

     _____

     If so, who? _____

12. Do you know that many Christians give much more than a tenth?

     _____

13. Is there a danger of our giving so much that God will reject us?

     _____

MATCH THE FOLLOWING

Below are eight quotations. Select the word from the list on the right that matches the quotation.

_____ 1. "Upon the first day of the week"   a. Purposefully

_____ 2. "Let every one of them"   b. Voluntarily

_____ 3. "as God has prospered"   c. Regularly

_____ 4. "That there be no gatherings"   d. Confidently

_____ 5. "Not begrudgingly nor of necessity   e. Cheerfully

_____ 6. "As he purposeth in his heart"   f. Personally

_____ 7. "God is able to make all grace abound   g. Proportionately
            toward you."
                                                      h. Preventively

_____ 8. "God loves a cheerful giver."

THINK! "THINK ON THESE THINGS"

1.   God's plan for financing the work of the church is by the free will offerings of the members.

   a.   How is the individual to get his money which enables him to give? THINK!_____

   b.   Would it be wrong for one to get money without working for it? THINK! _____

   c.   Could he invest some of the money he earns and earn more money? THINK!_____

   d.   When he does this should he give of this earning? THINK!

   _____

   e.   If a Christian inherits a sum of money should he give to the Lord a portion of that? THINK! _____

2.   Would it be right for the church to engage in some business enterprise to make money and use that money to finance the work of the church? THINK! _____
Explain your answer. _____

_____

3.   Members of the Lord's Church are to "lay by in store" upon the first day of the week. Would it be scriptural to take a collection on Wednesday night? THINK! _____
Why not? THINK! _____

_____

4.   Are Christians taught to give of their prosperity for other purposes than the common treasury of the church? THINK! _____

   a.   Name some other purpose of giving. _____

   _____

   b.   May this giving be done on some other day than "upon the first day of the week"? THINK! _____

5.   When each one gives, their gifts make up a common treasury.

    a.   Whose treasury is it? THINK! _____

    b.   Would it be right to call it the church treasury? THINK!_____

6.   For what should the money in this treasury be used? THINK!

    _____

7.   What does it mean to give "as God has prospered him"? THINK!

    _____

    _____

    a.   Does this mean everyone gives the same amount? THINK!_____

8.   What kind of giver does God love? THINK!_____

9.   Why is it "more blessed to give than to receive? THINK! _____

    _____

10.   Should everyone be taught and encouraged to give, regardless of how little they might have? THINK! _____

MEMORY—"THY WORD HAVE I HID IN MINE HEART"

1.   "Upon the first day of the week let every one of you lay by him in store, as God hath prospered him, that there be no gatherings when I come" (1 Corinthians 16:2).

2.   "Every man according as he purposeth in his heart, so let him give; not grudgingly, or of necessity: for God loveth a cheerful giver" (2 Corinthians 9:7).

3.   "...remember the words of the Lord Jesus, how he said, It is more blessed to give than to receive" (Acts 20:35).

A Study of Prayer

INTRODUCTION

1. Through the centuries the people of God have prayed unto our Father in heaven. Thus, we would expect to find the early disciples of Christ continuing prayer. (See Acts 2:42.)

2. In studying Christian worship we must give attention to the subject of prayer.

    a. It is one of the acts of worship.

    b. It played an important part in the lives of early disciples.

    c. It is our means of speaking to God.

I. Some general truths concerning prayer

    A. Prayer is properly addressed to God, our Father in heaven.

        1. Jesus taught men to pray to "our Father which art in heaven..." (Matthew 6:9)

            a. Example of Jesus praying: John 17:1, 5, 24; Matthew 26:39, 42; Luke 6:9

        2. The apostles taught men to pray to God, the Father (Ephesians 1:16-17; 3:14).

        3. Prayer has been addressed to Jesus:

            a. Stephen prayed unto Jesus (Acts 7:59-60)

            b. Paul may have prayed unto the Lord Jesus also (2 Corinthians 12:8)

                Note: This would be done only because they recognized the Lord as the mediator, who would intercede for them (John 16:23; Romans 8:34).

        4. Prayer is never addressed to the Holy Spirit.

            Note: The Spirit does make intercession for the saints (Romans 8:26-28).

    B. Prayer is offered in the name of Christ (John 14:13).

        1. This has not always been so:

       a.   In Old Testament times men did not pray through Christ.

       b.   During the personal ministry of Christ men did not pray in his name.

  2.   Jesus is now the one mediator between God and men (1 Timothy 2:5).

       a.   He ever liveth to make intercession for us (Hebrews 7:25).

II.   Kinds of prayers (1 Timothy 2:1-2)

  A.   Supplication (*deesis*): primarily a wanting, a need, then, an asking, entreaty, supplication, in the N.T. is always addressed to God and always rendered "supplication" in the R.V.

    1.   Used six times in the King James Version.

       a.   Acts 1:14—"These all continued with one accord in prayer and supplication..."

       b.   Ephesians 6:18—"Praying always with all prayer and supplication in the Spirit and watching thereunto with all perseverance and supplication..."

       c.   Philippians 4:6—"In everything by prayer and supplication with thanksgiving..."

       d.   1 Timothy 2:1—"...supplications and prayers..."

       e.   1 Timothy 5:5—"...continueth in supplications and prayers night and day."

    2.   In the R.V. supplication is rendered 12 times where it is "prayer" in K.J.

       a.   Luke 1:13—"Thy prayer is heard" (the angel to Zacharias).

       b.   Luke 2:27—Anna the prophetess...served God with fasting and prayers...

       c.   Luke 5:33—the disciples of John "fast often, and make prayers."

       d.   Romans 10:1—"My heart's desire and prayer to God."

       e.   2 Corinthians 1:11—"ye also helping together by prayer for us..."

       f.   2 Corinthians 9:14—"and by their prayer for you..."

g. Philippians 1:4—"always in every prayer of mine for you all making request with…"

h. Philippians 1:9—"for I know that this shall turn to my salvation through your prayer…" (for Paul while he was in bonds)

i. 2 Timothy 1:3—"I have remembrance of thee in my prayers night and day…"

j. Hebrews 5:7—"Who (Christ) in the days of his flesh, when he had offered up prayers and supplications with strong crying and tears."

k. James 5:16—"the effectual fervent prayer of a righteous man availeth much."

l. 1 Peter 3:12—"for the eyes of the Lord are over the righteous and his ears are open to their prayers…"

B. Prayers—the most general term, always used of prayer to God.

1. Matthew 21:22—"and all things, whatsoever ye shall ask in prayer, believing…"

2. Luke 6:12—Jesus went into the mountain "to pray, and continued all night in prayer."

3. James 5:17—Elias (Elijah) "prayed earnestly that it might not rain."

4. Ephesians 6:18—"Praying always with all prayer and supplication…"

5. Philippians 4:6—"In everything by prayer and supplication with thanksgiving let your request be made known unto God."

6. 1 Timothy 2:8—"I will therefore that men pray everywhere…"

7. 1 Timothy 5:5—Widow indeed "…continueth in supplications and prayers."

8. Hebrews 13:18—"Pray for us."

C. Intercession—primarily denotes a lighting upon, meeting with, then a conversation, hence a petition…it is a technical term for approaching a king, and so for approaching God in intercession. To plead with a person, either for or against. To make a petition on behalf of another.

1. Romans 8:26, 27—"The Spirit maketh intercession of us."

2. Romans 8:34—Christ is at the right hand of God, "who also maketh intercession for us."

3. Hebrews 7:25—"...he ever liveth to make intercession for us."

4. 1 Timothy 2:1—We should make "intercession" for others.

D. Giving of thanks—the expression of thankfulness.

1. Acts 24:3—(Tertullus) "with all thankfulness..."

2. 1 Corinthians 14:16—"How shall he say Amen at the end of giving thanks..."

3. 2 Corinthians 4:15—"For all things are for your sakes that the abundant grace might through the thanksgiving of many redound to the glory of God."

4. 2 Corinthians 9:11-12—"causeth through us thanksgiving to God..."

5. Philippians 4:6—"With thanksgiving let your requests be made known to God."

6. Colossians 2:7—"abounding therein with thanksgiving."

7. Colossians 4:2—"continue in prayer, and watch in the same with thanksgiving."

8. 1 Thessalonians 3:9—"For what thanks can we render to God again for you night and day..."

9. 1 Timothy 2:1—"supplications, prayers, intercessions and giving of thanks..."

10. 1 Timothy 4:3—"...which God hath created to be received with thanksgiving..."

11. 1 Timothy 4:4—"for every creature of God is good...if it be received with thanksgiving."

Note: Some were unthankful: Romans 1:21; Colossians 3:15

E. Petition—to ask.

1. 1 John 5:15—"and if we know that he hears us, whatsoever we ask, we know that we have the petitions that we desire of him."

2. From the same word as "ask."

F. Ask—to petition. There are two words from which "ask" is translated.

1. *Aiteo*—more frequently suggests the attitude of a supplicant, the petition of one who is lesser in position than he to whom the petition is made; e.g. in the case of men asking something from God (Matthew 7:7).

    a. A child from a parent (Matthew 7:9, 10).

    b. A subject from a king (Acts 12:20).

    c. Priests and people from Pilate (Luke 23:23).

    d. A beggar from a passer (Acts 3:2).

    e. With reference to petitioning God, this verb is found:

        (1) In Paul's epistles twice (Ephesians 3:20; Colossians 1:19).

        (2) In James four times (1:5, 6; 4:2, 3).

        (3) In 1 John five times (3:22; 5:14, 15 [twice], 16).

2. *Erotao*—more frequently suggests that the petitioner is on a footing of equality or familiarity with the person whom he requests.

    a. Used of a king in making requests from another king (Luke 14:32).

    b. Of the Pharisee who "desired" Christ that he would eat with him, and indication of the inferior concept he had of Christ (Luke 7:36; 11:37; John 9:15; John 18:19).

        Note: Jesus never used *aiteo* in the matter of making requests to the Father. "The consciousness of his dignity, of His potent and prevailing intercession, speaks out in this, that as often as he asks, or declares that He will ask anything of the Father, it is always *erotao*, an asking that is, upon equal terms. John 14:16; 16:26; 17:9, 15, 20, never *aiteo*, that he uses" (Quoted from *Synonym of the N.T.* by R. C. Trench; in *Expository Dictionary of New Testament Words*, W.E. Vine, Vol. 1, p. 79).

3. Observation:

    a. In John 16:23 both verbs are used:

        "in that day ye shall ask (*erotao*) me nothing"—on an equal basis.

"whatsoever he shall ask (*aiteo*) the Father"—the lesser asking of the greater.

    b.   John 14:14—"If ye shall ask anything in my name I will do it" is a request and *aiteo* is the verb—the lesser asking the greater.

    c.   1 John 5:16—"...a sin not unto death, he shall ask..." (*aiteo*)—lesser of the greater. "...There is a sin unto death...I do not say that he should pray..." (make request, R.V.)

G.   Request—denotes that which has been asked for.

    1.   Luke 23:24—requiring that he might be crucified..."Pilate gave sentence that it might be as they required" (R.V. says they were "urgent with loud voice").

    2.   Luke 21:36—"Watch ye therefore, and pray always..." (make supplication, R.V.)

    3.   Luke 22:32—"But I have prayed for thee" (made supplication, R.V.).

    4.   Acts 4:31—"and when they had prayed..."

    5.   Acts 8:22—"repent therefore of this thy wickedness and pray God..."

    6.   Acts 8:24—"Pray ye to the Lord for me."

    7.   Acts 10:2—"and prayed to God always."

    8.   Romans 1:10—"Making request..."

    9.   1 Thessalonians 3:10—"night and day praying exceedingly."

III.   Why we should continue in prayer

A.   For our daily needs

    1.   "Give us this day our daily bread" (Matthew 6:9-13, note v. 11).

    2.   Our Father in heaven knows how to give good things to them that ask him (Matthew 7:7-11).

B.   To obtain mercy.

    1.   We need His mercy in forgiveness when in weakness we yield to temptation.

C.   To find grace to help in time of need (Hebrews 4:16).

    1.   We should not try to "go it alone" (Proverbs 3:5-6).

    2.   When tempted to sin ask for God's help.

D. That we might lead a quiet and peaceable life in all godliness and honesty (1 Timothy 2:2).

  1. For this reason we should pray for those in positions of authority.

E. To evoke God's blessings upon each other (1 Timothy 2:2; Romans 10:1; 2 Timothy 1:3; Philippians 1:4; Colossians 13; 1 Thessalonians 1:2).

  1. For elders who oversee us

  2. For deacons who serve

  3. For gospel preachers

  4. For faithful brethren

  5. For those who are weak

  6. For parents and children

  7. For our young people

  8. For the aged disciples

F. To offer our praise and thanksgiving unto God (1 Thessalonians 5:18).

  1. "In everything give thanks; for this is the will of God in Christ concerning you."

G. On behalf of those who sin and ask our prayers.

  1. Simon asked Peter, "Pray ye to the Lord for me" (Acts 8:25).

  2. For those who sin a sin not unto death (1 John 5:16).

    a. A sin of which he repents and confesses to God.

H. For our own forgiveness (1 John 1:7-10; 2:1-2).

  1. God will forgive if we will repent and ask His forgiveness, and if we are of the disposition to forgive those who sin against us (Matthew 6:14-15).

I. For the salvation of others (Romans 10:1).

IV. How we should pray

A. We should study "how we should pray" from both the negative and positive point of view, i.e., we should pray "not this way," "but this way."

  1. NOT to be seen of men (Matthew 6:5), BUT in secret (Matthew 5:6)

2. NOT to be heard of men (Matthew 6:5), BUT to be heard by God (Matthew 6:9)

3. NOT with vain repetitions (Matthew 6:7), BUT with the spirit and the understanding (1 Corinthians 14:15-16)

4. NOT with unholy hands (1 Timothy 2:8), BUT with holy and righteous hands (1 Timothy 2:8)

5. NOT with wrath and doubting (1 Timothy 2:8), BUT in faith (Matthew 21:22; James 2:6)

6. NOT with a grudge in our hearts (Matthew 6:15), BUT with a spirit of forgiveness (Matthew 6:15)

7. NOT with a heart filled with pride (Luke 18:10-14), BUT in humility (Luke 18:10-14)

8. NOT in the name of men or of angels (1 Timothy 2:5), BUT in the name of Jesus Christ (John 16:23)

V.   Praying "in spirit and in truth"

A. Pray "in spirit"—proper attitude.

1. True worship must be rendered "in spirit."

2. This means we must be sincere in our prayers, "fervent prayers" (James 5:16)

a. This does not mean a prayer could not be written and read or memorized. However, to continually recite a memorized prayer may cause one to have a "form" but not be sincere in the reciting of the prayer.

b. A song may be read or memorized without becoming insincere.

c. Many preachers write their sermons and memorize them. Such does not remove the sincerity.

3. We should pray with an attitude of reverence and respect for Him before whom we come with our prayers.

a. Do not make prayers like a chat with a pal.

4. In public prayers the one leading the prayer must speak loudly enough to be heard by all and in words which all will understand, otherwise they cannot say "Amen" to his prayer (see 1 Corinthians 14:15-16).

5. Those who follow the leader must also maintain the proper attitude in order to pray "in spirit."

B. Pray "in truth"—as the New Testament teaches.

    1. True worship must be rendered "in truth."

    2. This means our prayers must be according to the New Testament teachings, i.e. directed unto God, asked in faith, in the name of Jesus, etc.

    3. Examples of prayers not in truth:

        a. Praying unto Mary, the Mother of Jesus.

            (1) Mary is not God and she is not a mediator between God and men (1 Timothy 2:5).

        b. Praying unto a "patron saint" as practiced by Catholicism.

        c. Praying contrary to the will of Christ or contrary to the New Testament teachings.

            (1) Sinners praying for salvation, i.e., mourner's bench system of religion.

        d. Asking God to forgive the sins of a brother who will not repent of and/or confess his sins (1 John 5:16; 1:9).

            Note: One may be very sincere (in spirit), but if his prayers are not "in truth" his worship is not true worship and will not be acceptable.

VI. The power of prayer

Note: We do not believe prayer can or will change the word of God or that which the word teaches. Prayer cannot make salvation possible for those who will not believe and obey God's will. But prayer has changed things, and there is still power in prayer (1 Peter 3:12).

A. Examples of the power of prayer.

    1. Elijah and his prayer (James 5:17-18)

        a. The very purpose of this reference is to illustrate the power of prayer.

    2. Moses and his prayer (Exodus 32:31-32)

        a. God had intended to "consume" the people and make of Moses a great nation (cf. vs. 9).

        b. Moses prayed for God to forgive the sin of the people (vs. 32).

        c.   Only those who had sinned were punished.

  B.   There is power in the prayers of the righteous.

      1.   The effectual fervent prayer of a righteous man availeth much (1 Peter 3:13).

      2.   Let us not question or doubt the effectiveness of prayer.

CONCLUSION

1.   Are you continuing in prayer?

2.   Will you begin to pray every day? To ask God to help you be a better Christian?

3.   Will you begin trying to convert someone who is lost, and ask God's help in this great work?

Lesson 12

Some Questions on Prayer

WHAT DOES THE SCRIPTURE SAY?

References: Matthew 6:9; Matthew 21:22; Luke 6:12; John 14:14;
1 Corinthians 14:15; Ephesians 6:18; Philippians 4:6; 1 Timothy 2:5;
1 Timothy 5:5; Hebrews 7:25; James 1:5-6; James 5:16; 1 Peter 3:12

1. "After this _____ therefore, _____ ye; Our _____ which are in heaven, Hallowed be thy name."

2. "And all things, whatsoever ye shall _____ in _____ believing, ye shall _____."

3. "And it came to pass in those days, that _____ went out into a mountain to _____, and continued all night in _____ to God."

4. "If ye shall _____ any thing in my _____, I will do it."

5. "What is it then? I will _____ with the _____ and I will _____ with the _____ also..."

6. "Praying always with all _____ and _____ in the Spirit."

7. "Be careful for nothing; but in every thing by _____ and supplication with _____ let your requests be make known unto _____."

8. "For there is one God, and one _____ between God and men, the man _____ _____."

9. "Now she that is a widow indeed, and desolate, _____ in god, and continueth in _____ and _____ night and day."

10. "Wherefore he is able also to save them to the uttermost that
_____ unto God _____ _____, seeing he ever
liveth to make _____ for them."

11. "If any of you lack _____, let him _____ of God, that
giveth to all men liberally, and upbraideth not; and it shall be
_____ him. But let him ask _____ _____ noting
wavering..."

12. "_____ your faults one to another, and _____ one
for another, that ye may be healed. The _____ prayer of a
_____ man availeth much."

13. "For the _____ of the Lord are over the _____ and his
_____ are open unto their _____ but the face of the
Lord is against them that do evil."

BRIEF ANSWERS

1. To whom should prayer be addressed? _____

2. Who should pray? _____

3. The ears of the Lord are opened unto the prayers of whom?

_____

4. Who is the mediator between God and men? _____

5. If our worship is acceptable how must our prayers be made?

_____

TALK TIME—DISCUSSION

1. Jesus taught his disciples to pray (Matthew 6:5-15).

   a. They were not to pray as the hypocrites. How did the
   hypocrites pray?_____

   _____

b. What does it mean: "When thou prayest, enter into thy closet"?

_____

_____

c. For what did they pray? _____

_____

2. Jesus was a man of prayer. List below two of the prayers of Jesus. Give the reference and something about each prayer.

a. _____

_____

b. _____

_____

3. Read 1 Timothy 2:1-2. How many kinds of prayers are mentioned?

_____

Name them. _____

_____

4. Subject: supplications

a. What are supplications?_____

_____

b. Does the R.V. use the word supplication in some instances where the K.J. uses prayer?_____ How many times? _____

5. Subject: intercessions

a. Define the word. _____

_____

b. What is the difference between intercessions and supplications? _____

_____

c. Two passages teach that Christ makes intercession for us. What are they? _____

What do they mean? _____

_____

d.   Do Christians make intercessions for other men?_____
Cite the reference. _____

6.   Subject: giving of thanks

a.   Define the expression. _____

_____

b.   How does this differ from intercession?_____

_____

c.   How does it differ from supplications? _____

_____

d.   Name some things for which we should give thanks. _____

_____

_____

e.   Give an example of unthankfulness. _____

_____

_____

7.   Subject: petition

a.   What does it mean? _____

_____

b.   Show the difference between petition and "giving of thanks."

_____

_____

8.   Subject: to ask (Matthew 7:7)

a.   "Ask" is translated from two different words. Give those words
and the meaning of each to show the difference between them.

(1)   _____

(2)   _____

b. Give an example of "ask" when it is the lesser asking of the greater._____

_____

c. Give an example of "ask" when the petitioner is on a footing of equality._____

_____

d. Read John 16:23. Both words are in this passage, but appear as "ask" in the English. Discuss the difference. _____

_____

_____

9. Subject: making request

a. Define "request."_____

_____

b. Should Christians make their requests known to God? _____

10. Subject: beseech

a. Define the word. _____

_____

b. How does this word differ from the word "ask?" _____

_____

11. List nine things which show why we should continue in prayer. Give a reference for each.

a. _____

b. _____

c. _____

d. _____

e. _____

f. _____

g.   _____

h.   _____

i.   _____

12.   What example is cited to show the power of prayer?_____
_____

a.   For what did Elijah pray? _____

b.   Was his prayer a selfish prayer?_____

c.   Was there power in his prayer?_____

d.   What was the purpose for such a prayer? _____
_____

e.   What other example is mentioned in the outline?_____
_____

f.   What is said of the effectual fervent prayer of a righteous man?
_____

(1) Do you believe this?_____

(2) Do you pray? _____

13.   Discuss praying in spirit and in truth.

a.   What does it mean to pray "in spirit"?_____
_____

b.   What kind of attitude should we have when we approach God
in prayer? _____

c.   How does one pray "in truth"? _____
_____

d.   Give two examples of praying but not praying in truth.

(1) _____

(2) _____

14. Be prepared to tell how we should and should not pray.

How We Should	How We Should Not
_____	_____
_____	_____
_____	_____
_____	_____
_____	_____
_____	_____
_____	_____

THINK! "THINK ON THESE THINGS"

1. When Jesus taught his disciples how to pray (Matthew 6:5-15), how do we know this was only a model prayer for them and not a prayer by Jesus? THINK! _____
   _____

   a. What condition did Jesus give for our being forgiven of our trespasses? THINK!_____

   b. Should we still pray "Thy kingdom come"? THINK! _____

   c. When we pray "give us this day our daily bread," does this mean we should not work to obtain it? THINK!_____

   d. When we pray for those who are lost that they might be saved, is there anything more we can do for them? THINK! _____

2. Who are some for whom we should pray? THINK! List several of them. THINK! _____
   _____

3. When we ask of the Father in heaven is this the lesser asking of the greater? THINK!_____
   Does this have to do with praying "in spirit"? THINK!_____

4. What does "amen" mean at the close of a prayer? THINK!_____
    _____

5. After reading 1 Corinthians 14:16, what would you say is required in order for one to say "amen" to the prayer of another? THINK!
    _____
    _____

    a. What lesson should all brethren who lead the prayers learn from this? THINK! _____
        _____

    b. What do you think: Do the brethren say "amen" to the prayers of others as much as they should? THINK! _____

6. Does reading a prayer or memorizing a prayer for a given occasion indicate that one is not praying "in spirit"? THINK! _____

    a. What about memorizing a song? THINK! _____

    b. What would be the danger of repeating the same memorized prayer again and again? THINK! _____
        _____

7. In the parable of the Pharisee and the publican who went up into the temple to pray (Luke 18:10-14), what kind of man was the Pharisee? THINK! _____

    a. How would you make an application of this today? THINK!
        _____
        _____

    b. Could a religious man who worships regularly, lives a good clean life and gives to the needy have his prayers rejected? THINK! _____

    c. Is it possible for members of the church to think too highly of themselves? THINK! _____

8. In the same parable (Luke 18:10-14) what kind of man was the publican? THINK! _____

a. Is it possible that some whom we think are not so righteous may be more acceptable to God than others whom we think are very righteous? THINK!_____

b. Does this relate to praying "in spirit and in truth"? THINK!

_____

9. What does it mean to "continue in prayer" or to "pray without ceasing"? THINK! _____

_____

a. Does it mean one should pray all the time? THINK! _____

b. If he prayed all the time when would he work? THINK!_____

_____

PRAY—FOR WHAT?

In the column on the left are some for whom we should pray. On the blanks opposite these, write some things we should ask for them.

1. Rulers _____

2. Our children _____

3. The lost _____

4. Elders _____

5. The sick _____

6. Preachers _____

7. One another _____

8. Those who persecute
us or despitefully use us _____

9. Enemies _____

10. Self _____

MEMORY—"THY WORD HAVE I HID IN MINE HEART"

1.   "What is it then? I will pray with the spirit, and I will pray with the understanding also: I will sing with the spirit, and I will sing with the understanding also" (1 Corinthians 14:15).

2.   "Confess your faults one to another, and pray one for another, that ye may be healed. The effectual fervent prayer of a righteous man availeth much" (James 5:16).

3.   "I exhort therefore, that, first of all, supplications, prayers, intercessions, and giving of thanks, be made for all men" (1 Timothy 2:1).

Praying in the Name of Jesus

INTRODUCTION

1.   Whatever we do, we must do it "in the name of the Lord Jesus," giving thanks to God by him (Colossians 3:17).

2.   For several years we have noticed that many denominational preachers do not pray "in the name of Christ." Christ has been completely omitted from the prayers of many, with their prayers being addressed unto God in Heaven and closed with "amen." Some brethren have taught that it is not necessary to mention Christ in our prayers, but I have never known any who omitted him.

   a.   It is said, "in the name of" means by the authority of, and functions performed in the name of Christ involve something DONE, not something said.

   b.   Examples:

      (1)   Preaching "in the name of Christ" does not mean that one is continually saying "in the name of Christ."

      (2)   Baptizing "in the name of Christ" does not mean there is a certain ceremony to be said but refers to what is being done.

3.   Define "in the name of":

   a.   Thayer: "relying or resting on the mane of Christ, rooted (so to speak) in his name. i.e. mindful of Christ and in reliance on the word which invites us to him" (John 14:13) (*Greek-English Lexicon*, p. 448).

   b.   W.E. Vine: the phrase stands "for all that a name implies, of authority, character, rank, majesty, power, excellence, etc., of everything that the name covers...in recognition of authority..." (*Expository Dictionary of the N.T. Words*, Vol. III, p. 100)

4.   The religion Jesus taught is not one of ceremonies and rituals:

   a.   No ceremony for baptism, though the "Jesus Only" groups contend for such.

       b.   No ceremony for prayer, and I do not contend for one.

5.   I do believe one should in some way make known the fact that he is praying to God through Jesus Christ.

       a.   He may say "in the name of Christ," "in the name of our Lord," "in the name of our Savior," "Through Christ," "in Jesus' name," etc.

6.   Jews, Modernists, and Masons do not pray in the name of Christ.

       a.   Why should any Christian want to leave Christ out of his prayers?

       b.   Why should any Christian be connected with any organizations that would forbid him to pray in the name of Christ?

I.   What Jesus taught

    A.   On the night before his death, Jesus taught the disciples to pray in his name.

       1.   "Whatsoever ye shall ask in my name, that will I do..." (John 14:13)

       2.   "If ye shall ask anything in my name, I will do it" (John 14:14).

       3.   "That whatsoever ye shall ask of the Father in my name, he may give it to you" (John 15:15).

       4.   "Whatsoever ye shall ask the Father in my name, he will give it to you...Hitherto have ye asked nothing in my name...At that day ye shall ask in my name" (John 16:23-27).

    B.   Before that night Jesus had taught them to pray:

       1.   "After this manner therefore pray ye..." (Matthew 6:9-13)

    C.   Now he says, "Hitherto have ye asked nothing in my name" (John 16:24).

       1.   "Hitherto" means, "up to this time, as yet, up to now."

       2.   Jesus is saying: Up to this time ye have asked nothing in my name.

       3.   Question: Had the disciples prayed during the past three years as Jesus taught them?

       4.   If "in my name" means only "by my authority," we must conclude that they had not prayed at all as Jesus had taught them.

          a.   Jesus taught them HOW to pray, but they did not pray... Who can believe it?

II. Why we pray "in the name of Christ"

    A. In the model prayer Jesus did not teach men to pray in his name (Matthew 6:9-13).

        1. Why?

            a. At that time he was not the mediator between God and man (1 Timothy 2:5).

            b. He had not ascended unto the Father (John 20:17).

    B. Not until the time for his death came did he teach them to pray in his name.

        1. In his death the middle wall of partition between Jews and Gentiles would be broken down (Ephesians 2:14-16).

        2. In his death the old law would be nailed to the cross (Colossians 2:14-16).

        3. He would be raised from the dead and ascend into heaven to become the high priest for God's people (Hebrews 4:14-16).

            a. He could not fill this office while on earth (cf. Hebrews 8:14).

            b. So he fulfilled the old covenant and became the mediator of a better covenant (Hebrews 8:6-13; 10:9-10).

        4. Not until the night before his death did he teach them to "ask in my name," because "I go to my Father" (John 14:12-13).

    C. We pray "in his name" because:

        1. He is our high priest (Hebrews 4:14-16).

        2. He is the one mediator between God and men (1 Timothy 2:5).

            a. Before he ascended he was not the mediator.

            b. Up to this time they asked nothing in his name (John 16:23).

        3. We are commanded to give thanks to God by him (Colossians 3:17).

        4. He is our intercessor (Romans 8:34).

        5. He is our advocate (1 John 2:1-2).

        6. We are to glorify the Father in the Son (John 14:13).

III. Things to consider

A. The expression "in the name of Christ" means more than "by the authority of Christ."

    1. It signifies that he is our mediator, high priest, intercessor, advocate.

B. Consider these things:

    1. There is one mediator (1 Timothy 2:5).

        a. Do we need this mediator?

        b. Can we make "supplication, prayers, intercessions, giving of thanks" as well without him?

        c. If so, is Jesus filling an unnecessary position?

    2. Jesus is our high priest (Hebrews 4:13-16).

        a. "All things are naked and opened" before God's eye.

        b. We have an high priest who can be touched with the feelings of our infirmities.

        c. Can we "obtain mercy" from our high priest if we do not acknowledge him?

        d. Can we "find grace to help" from our high priest if we by-pass him when we pray?

    3. Jesus said, "in that day ye shall ask me nothing...whatsoever ye ask the Father in my name, he will give it" (John 16:13).

        a. During his personal ministry they asked many things of Jesus.

        b. Now they must ask the Father in the name of Jesus.

        c. Would it be just as well to ask the Father without the name of Jesus?

    4. Jesus said, "Whatsoever ye shall ask in my name, that will I do, that the Father may be glorified in the son" (John 14:13).

        a. If we ask without mentioning His name how can the Father be glorified in the Son?

        b. Can we glorify the Father in the name Christian if we do not wear the name (1 Peter 4:16)?

    5. Paul said, "...giving thanks to God and the Father by him" (Colossians 3:17).

        a. "Giving thanks through Him to God the Father" (NASB).

    b. Can we omit him and give thanks to God? What about the Jews?

  6. If "in the name of" means only "by the authority of" Christ, please explain: "Hitherto have ye asked nothing in my name" (John 16:24).

CONCLUSION

1. While there is no ceremony connected with prayer, we should in all of our prayers make known the fact that we are praying through Jesus Christ.

2. When we mention Christ in our prayers:

    a. We glorify the Father in the Son.

    b. We profess our faith in Christ.

    c. We acknowledge the position and function of our Lord.

3. Don't leave Christ out of your prayers.

Lesson 14

Some Questions About Praying in the Name of Jesus

WHAT DOES THE SCRIPTURE SAY?

References: Matthew 6:9; John 14:12-13; John 14:14; John 15:16; John 16:23; John 16:24; Romans 8:34; Colossians 3:17; 1 Timothy 2:5; 1 John 2:1-2

1. "After this manner there _____ ye: Our _____ which art in _____, Hallowed be thy name."

2. "And whatsoever ye shall ask _____ _____ _____, that will I do, that the _____ may be glorified in the Son."

3. "If ye shall ask any thing _____ _____ _____, I will _____ it."

4. "...that whatsoever ye shall ask of the _____ in _____, he may give it you."

5. "And in that day ye shall _____ me nothing. Verily, verily I say unto you, Whatsoever ye shall _____ the Father in _____ name, he will give it you."

6. "Hitherto have ye _____ nothing in my _____: ask and ye shall _____, that your joy may be full."

7. "For what the _____ could not do, in that it was weak through the _____, God sending his own Son in the likeness of _____ _____, and for sin, condemned in the flesh."

8. "And whatsoever ye do in _____ or _____, do all in the _____ of the Lord Jesus, giving _____ to God and the Father by him."

9. "For there is one _____, and one _____ between God and men, the man Christ Jesus."

10. "...And if any man sin, we have an _____ with the Father, _____ _____ the righteous: And he is the _____ for our sins: and not for ours only, but also for the _____ of the whole world."

TALK TIME—DISCUSSION

1. Be prepared to discuss the expression "in the name of."

   a. What does it mean? _____
   _____

   b. What is a "ceremony"? _____
   _____

   c. What is a "ritual"? _____
   _____

   d. Is praying "in the name of Christ" merely a ceremony?_____
   A ritual? _____

2. Read John 14:12-14.

   a. When did this teaching take place? Give the time in the life of Christ, i.e., beginning of personal ministry, middle of personal ministry, or close of personal ministry. _____
   _____

   b. Where did Jesus say he was going?_____

   c. Why did Jesus say, "Whatsoever ye shall ask in my name, that will I do"?_____

   d. What did Jesus promise to do for the disciples "If ye shall ask anything in my name"?_____
   _____

3.   Read John 15:14-16.

   a.   Was this spoken on the same night as the teaching in
        John 14:12-14? _____

   b.   Of whom were the disciples to ask? _____

   c.   In whose name were they to ask it? _____

4.   Read John 16:23-27.

   a.   When Jesus said, "and in that day ye shall ask me nothing"
        (v. 23) what day is "that day" (see vs. 21-22)? _____

        _____

   b.   In "that day" they were to ask of whom? _____

   c.   In whose name were they to ask? _____

   d.   What does "hitherto" mean (v. 24)?_____

   e.   Had the disciples been praying "in the name of Christ"? _____

   f.   What were the disciples to do "at that day" (v. 26)?_____

   g.   What did Jesus say he would do for them? _____

        _____

5.   Subject: the model prayer (Matthew 6:9-13)

   a.   At what time in the personal ministry of Jesus was this model
        prayer taught? _____

   b.   Was Jesus teaching his disciples to pray? _____

   c.   Unto whom were they to pray?_____

   d.   At this time were they taught to pray in the name of Christ?

        _____

6.   Subject: Christ our "High Priest" (Ephesians 2:14-16; Hebrews 4:14-16;
      8:6-13; 10:9-10)

   a.   What was the "middle wall of partition" that was abolished
        when Christ died on the cross?_____

b.   Under the law of Moses who were the priests? _____
_____

Who were the High Priests? _____
_____

c.   While Jesus lived on earth was he a priest? _____
Was he the high priest? _____

d.   Why could he not be a priest while on earth? _____
_____

e.   "He taketh away the first, that he may establish the second"
(Hebrews 10:9-10). First and second what?_____

f.   How do we know that Jesus can be "touched with the feelings
of our infirmities? _____
_____

g.   Does this make him a better high priest? _____

7.   Praying "in the name of Jesus." List four reasons why we should
pray "in the name of Christ." Give a reference for each.

a.   _____

b.   _____

c.   _____

d.   _____

8.   Subject: Christ our advocate (1 John 2:1-2)

a.   Define "advocate"._____
_____

b.   Who is our advocate? _____

c.   Of what benefit is an advocate?_____
_____

9.   Read Colossians 3:17.

a. What does "do all in the name of the Lord" mean? _____

_____

b. What does it mean to give thanks unto God "by him"? By
whom? _____

c. How does the NASB (New American Standard Bible) read?

_____

10. Subject: Christ the mediator (1 Timothy 2:15)

a. What is a mediator? _____

_____

b. Has Christ always been the mediator between God and men?

_____

c. When did he become the mediator? _____

_____

11. Name some who do not pray in the name of Jesus. _____

_____

_____

THINK! "THINK ON THESE THINGS"

1. Jesus taught the disciples how to pray (Matthew 6:9-13).

a. Would you say they obeyed his teaching? THINK! _____

b. If so did they pray? THINK! _____

c. At this time were they to pray "in the name of Christ"? THINK!

_____

2. On the night before his death he taught then to ask "in my name"
(John 16:23-24). He said, "Hitherto (or up to this time) have ye asked
nothing in my name," but, "At that day ye shall ask in my name"
(John 16:24, 26).

a. Had they been praying during the past three years? _____

    b. Had they prayed as Jesus taught them (Matthew 6:9-13)? _____

    c. Did they pray by his authority before that time? THINK! _____

    d. If "in my name" merely beans "by my authority" were they praying "in the name of Christ" before his death?_____

    e. How does this show that "in the name of" does not mean just "by the authority of" in this passage? THINK!_____

        _____

        _____

3.   Whatever we do in word or deed we are to do "in the name of the Lord Jesus" (Colossians 3:17).

    a. Does this mean we are to go around saying "in the name of Christ" do this or that? THINK! _____

4.   The Orthodox Jew, the Masons, the infidels do not pray to God through Christ. Why? THINK! _____

    Are their prayers acceptable to God? THINK!_____

5.   Many sectarian preachers do not mention Christ in their prayers. They pray unto God but omit the name of Christ.

    a. Since Christ is the "one mediator" between God and men, can men pray "in truth" without praying through Christ? THINK!

        _____

    b. Is the position of a mediator an unnecessary and unprofitable position? THINK! _____

6.   Must all prayers end with the expression "in the name of Jesus, Amen"? THINK!_____

    What are some other expressions that may be used to set forth the idea of praying through Christ? THINK!_____

    _____

    _____

    _____

7. What is necessary to pray "in the name of Jesus Christ"? THINK!

    _____

8. Knowing that we have a high priest who can be touched with our feelings, we are exhorted to "come boldly unto the throne of grace, that we may obtain mercy, and find grace to help in time of need" (Hebrews 4:16), Can our high priest help us if we bypass him when we pray? THINK! _____

9. Jesus said, "...Whatsoever ye ask the Father, in my name, he will give it" (John 16:23). Would the Father give it just as readily if we did not ask in the name of Jesus? THINK!_____

10. Some argue that they can pray "in the name of Jesus" without mentioning his name. Is this possible? THINK! _____
    They say "in the name of" means "by the authority of" and they claim to pray as Jesus taught. Question: Did Jesus teach his disciples to pray "in my name"? THINK! _____
    Why would one want to omit Christ from his prayers? THINK!

    _____

    _____

11. The night before his death Jesus taught the disciples to pray "in my name." Six times he told them this (John 14:13; 14:14; 15:16; 16:23; 16:24; 16:26).

    a. Does the repetition of this appear to emphasize the lesson he is teaching? THINK!_____

    b. If they were to pray exactly as they had been praying, why did Jesus tell them to ask "in my name"? THINK! _____

        _____

12. Jesus said, "Whatsoever ye ask in my name, that will I do, that the Father may be glorified in the Son" (John 14:13).

    a. If we ask without mentioning his name how can the Father be glorified "in the Son"? THINK! _____

        _____

b.   Can we glorify the Father in the name Christian (1 Peter 4:16) if we do not wear that name? THINK! _____

13.   Acceptable worship must be rendered "in spirit and in truth" (John 4:24). Can one pray "in spirit" without praying through Christ? THINK!_____

Can one pray "in truth" without praying through Christ? THINK!

_____

In a public assembly how can those present know we are praying "in the name of" Christ if Christ is not mentioned in the prayer? THINK!_____

WHAT YOU SHOULD LEARN FROM THIS LESSON

1.   There is one mediator between God and men, Christ Jesus.

2.   We are to pray unto God in the name of Christ.

3.   When we pray through Christ, we glorify the Father in the Son, we profess our faith in Christ, and we acknowledge our faith in Christ.

4.   Do not leave Christ out of your prayers.

MEMORY—"THY WORD HAVE I HID IN MINE HEART"

1.   "For there is one God, and one mediator between God and men, the man Christ Jesus" (1 Timothy 2:5).

2.   "And whatsoever ye shall ask in my name, that will I do, that the Father may be glorified in the Son" (John 14:13).

Music in Worship

INTRODUCTION

1. Through the centuries man has used music in his worship, whether worshipping the true God, or the idols made by men.

2. This lesson is designed to help the student determine the kind of music to be used by Christians in worship unto God. Therefore, we must determine the kind of music taught in the New Testament. Remember that any appeal made unto the Old Testament, the law and the prophets, would fail to accomplish this purpose, since the law ended when Jesus died on the cross (Colossians 2:14-17; Ephesians 2:14-17).

I. Music defined

    A. Understanding the term. Before we study music we must be sure we understand the meaning of the word, else we may not have the same thing in mind when we think of music.

        1. Example: People who visit our services frequently say, "Oh, I did not realize you people do not use music in worship." Or, they may ask, "Why don't you have music in your church?" When they say music they have in mind instrumental music. However, music involves more than mechanical instruments.

    B. Music defined: "The science or art of pleasing, expressive, or intelligible combination of tones, the art of making such combinations. Sound having rhythm and melody" (Webster).

II. Kinds of music

    A. Vocal music, i.e. music made with the human vocal system.

        1. God created man with a vocal system capable of speaking and of singing. The degree of musical ability, natural or acquired, may vary from person to person, yet most people are capable of making music with the vocal system. God has made us so.

        2. Vocal music consists of singing, humming, whistling, yodeling, and anything else that would constitute a

"combination of pleasing tones" made with the vocal system. Of these possibilities, singing is the most common.

B. Mechanical instrumental music, i.e., music made by the use of mechanical instruments or devices.

1. Mechanical instruments of music date back to the eighth generation of man: "Jabel was the father of all such as handle the harp and organ" (Genesis 4:21).

2. Mechanical instruments are grouped under different headings: string, wind, reed, brass, percussion. Each of these have numerous kinds of instruments, but all are properly classified as mechanical instruments of music.

3. Note: There are only two kinds of music made by men—vocal and instrumental. There are other kinds of music in the world, such as the birds singing, the rippling waters of a mountain stream, but these could hardly be the kind of music Christians use in worshipping God.

III. Does God have a choice regarding the kind of music Christians use in worshipping him?

A. God's choice in a matter may be seen by the use of a specific in contrast to a generic term. Examples of the choice of God:

1. For the ark God chose "gopher wood" (Genesis 6:14). Wood is a generic term including all kinds of wood. There are many kinds of wood. If God had said unto Noah, "Make thee an ark of wood," then any kind of wood would have been acceptable. God's choice was seen in the specific "gopher wood." When God chose "gopher wood" for the ark he did not have to say, "Thou shalt not use oak, elm, hickory, ash, etc." All of these were excluded by the specific choice of God.

CHART #1
Wood

| OAK | ELM | HICKORY | GOPHER | ASH | WALNUT | CEDAR |

2. For the passover sacrifice God chose "a lamb" (Exodus 12:3-5). Animal is a generic term including all kinds of animals. If God had said, "Take to them every man an animal," then any kind of animal would have been acceptable. But the

children of Israel were restricted to one kind of animal, for God said, "They shall take to them every man a lamb..." This excluded all other animals. But God was even more specific. When he said "From the sheep, or from the goats" he excluded other kinds of animals; "without blemish" would exclude those with blemishes or imperfections (blind, crippled, diseased, etc.); "a male" would exclude the females; "of the first year" would exclude those animals that were older; God had a choice and his choice was seen in the commandment given.

CHART #2
Animal

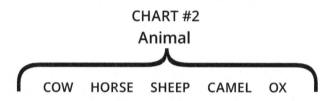

COW   HORSE   SHEEP   CAMEL   OX

CHART #3
Sheep or Goat

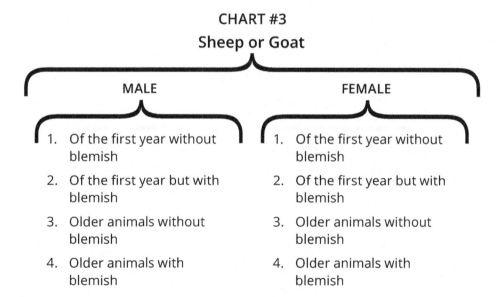

MALE	FEMALE
1. Of the first year without blemish	1. Of the first year without blemish
2. Of the first year but with blemish	2. Of the first year but with blemish
3. Older animals without blemish	3. Older animals without blemish
4. Older animals with blemish	4. Older animals with blemish

3. God's choice regarding the kind of music to be used by Christians in worship is seen in the specific instructions he has given. The words "sing," "singing," and "sung" indicate his choice. The word music is a generic term, just as wood and animal are generic terms. If God had commanded that Christians "make music" unto him, then any kind of music would be acceptable. However when he specifies singing, this shows the choice of God and excludes other kinds of music.

a. Just like "a sheep" excluded other kinds of animals, and "gopher wood" excluded other kinds of wood, even so, "singing" excludes other kinds of music.

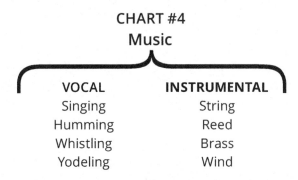

CHART #4
Music

VOCAL	INSTRUMENTAL
Singing	String
Humming	Reed
Whistling	Brass
Yodeling	Wind

b. If God had said, "make vocal music in worship unto me," then any kind of vocal music would be acceptable. But God specified a particular kind of vocal music and excludes all other kinds of vocal music, i.e. humming, whistling, yodeling. God did not say vocal music, he specified the kind—singing.

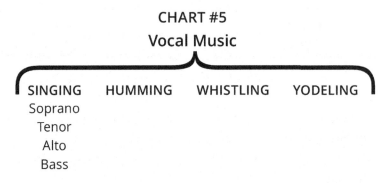

CHART #5
Vocal Music

SINGING	HUMMING	WHISTLING	YODELING
Soprano			
Tenor			
Alto			
Bass			

Compare this to the passover sacrifice "from the sheep of from the goats" excludes all other animals. But many sheep and goats were excluded by the specific "a male," "of the first year," "without blemish" (see chart #3). Many other males were excluded. All females were excluded when God specified male. Even so, singing excludes all other kinds of vocal music (see chart #5).

B. God's choice seen in the scriptures. Music in worship is found ten times in the New Testament. Notice the kind of music God has specified:

1. "They had **sung** a hymn..." (Matthew 26:30)
2. "They had **sung** a hymn..." (Mark 14:26)
3. "Were **singing** hymns unto God" (Acts 16:25).
4. "And **sing** unto thy name" (Romans 15:9).
5. "I will **sing** with the spirit..." (1 Corinthians 14:15)
6. "I will **sing** with the understanding also" (1 Corinthians 14:15).
7. "**Singing** and making melody in your heart..." (Ephesians 5:19)
8. "**Singing** with grace in your hearts to the Lord" (Colossians 3:16).
9. "In the midst of the church will I **sing** praise unto thee" (Hebrews 2:12).
10. "Is any merry? Let him **sing** psalms" (James 5:13).

Note: There are other references in the New Testament to music, but they do not pertain to the music to be used by Christians in worshipping God. For this reason they are not included in this study.

CONCLUSION

1. From these references we should be able to see that God has a choice regarding music used by Christians in their worship unto Him.

2. Study chart #6 and notice that God chose a particular kind of animal for a sacrifice. If you are able to see that His choice of a male lamb, of the first year, without blemish, would exclude all other animals, then you should be able to study chart #7 and see how God's choice of a particular kind of vocal music would exclude all other kinds of music.

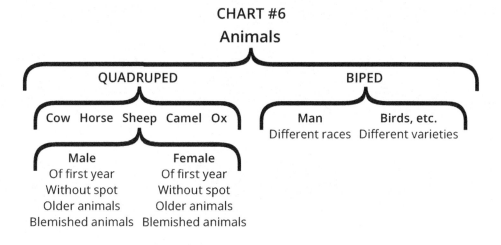

CHART #6
Animals

QUADRUPED — BIPED

Cow Horse Sheep Camel Ox   Man   Birds, etc.
                                 Different races   Different varieties

Male   Female
Of first year   Of first year
Without spot   Without spot
Older animals   Older animals
Blemished animals   Blemished animals

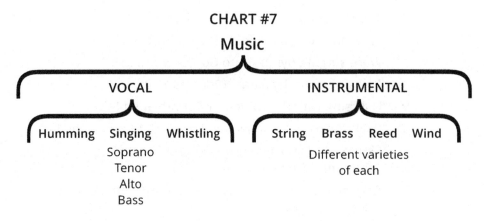

CHART #7

Music

VOCAL — INSTRUMENTAL

Humming   Singing   Whistling   String   Brass   Reed   Wind

Soprano   Different varieties
Tenor   of each
Alto
Bass

3.   We must have respect for the will of God and not be guilty of adding to or taking from His will (see Revelation 22:18-19).

Some Questions About Music

WHAT DOES THE SCRIPTURE SAY?

References: Genesis 6:14; Exodus 12:3; Exodus 3:5; Genesis 4:21;
Colossians 2:14; Matthew 26:30; Acts 16:25; Romans 15:9;
1 Corinthians 14:15; Ephesians 5:19; Colossians 3:16; Hebrews 2:12;
James 5:13

1. "Make thee an _____ of _____ wood; _____ shalt thou make in the ark, and shalt _____ it within and without with _____."

2. "Speak ye unto all the congregations of Israel, saying, In the _____ _____ of this month they shall take to them every man a _____, according to the house of their fathers, a _____ for a house:"

3. "And he said, Draw not nigh hither: put off they _____ from off they _____; for the place whereon thou standest is _____ _____."

4. "And his brother's name was _____ he was the father of all such as handle the _____ and _____."

5. "Blotting out the handwriting of _____ that was against us, which was _____ to us, and took it out of the way, _____ it to the cross."

6. "And when they had _____ a _____, they went out into the mount of Olives."

7. "And at _____ Paul and Silas prayed, and sang _____ unto God: and the prisoners heard them."

8. "And that the Gentiles might _____ God for his _____; as it is written, For this cause I will _____ to thee among the Gentiles, and sing unto thy name."

9. "What is it then? I will pray with the spirit, and I will pray with the understanding also; I will _____ with the _____ and I will _____ with the understanding also."

10. "Speaking to yourselves in _____ and _____ and _____ _____ singing and making _____ in your heart to the Lord."

11. "Let the word of Christ dwell in you richly in all wisdom teaching and admonishing one another in _____ and _____ and _____ _____ singing with _____ in your heart to the Lord."

12. "Saying, I will _____ thy name unto my brethren, in the midst of the church will I _____ _____ unto thee."

13. "Is any among you _____? Let him _____. Is any _____? Let him sing _____."

UNDERSTANDING WORDS

1. Define music._____

    _____

2. Define generic. _____

    _____

3. Define specific. _____

    _____

4. What is vocal music? _____

    _____

5. What is mechanical music? _____

    _____

6.   Define choice. _____

       _____

  TALK TIME—DISCUSSION

1.   What do people sometimes say which shows that they think of
       music as being only instrumental? _____

       _____

       _____

2.   There are two kinds of music made by men. What are they? _____

       _____

3.   Name some different kinds of vocal music. _____

       _____

4.   When God has a choice in any matter how do we learn of his
       choice? _____

       _____

5.   Did God have a choice regarding the kind of wood to be used in
       building the ark? _____
       What was his choice? _____
       How did Noah know of God's choice? _____

       _____

6.   Did God have a choice of animals to be used in the passover
       sacrifice (Exodus 12:3-5)? _____
       What was his choice? _____
       How did the children of Israel know of God's choice? _____

       _____

7.   Does God have a choice of music to be used by Christians in
       worship?_____
       What is his choice? _____
       How do we know of God's choice?_____

       _____

GENERIC AND SPECIFIC

Understanding generic and specific terms is very helpful in learning truth. Remember: generic is general, including an entire group or class, while specific is explicit, setting forth one of the group or class.

1.   From chart 1

    a.   What is the generic?_____

    b.   What is a specific?_____

    c.   How many specifics are named? _____

    d.   Are oak, elm, and gopher wood of the same class of kind?

       _____

    e.   How does the choosing of a specific differ from choosing the generic? In this instance the specific is gopher. The generic is wood. _____

       _____

    f.   How did choosing gopher wood exclude the use of other kinds of wood? _____

       _____

2.   From chart 2

    a.   What is the generic?_____

    b.   What are some specifics? _____

    c.   Does each specific have the same relation to the generic?_____

    d.   Did God command the use of a generic or a specific?_____

    e.   How does the choosing of a specific differ from the choosing of the generic in regards to the sacrifice? _____

       _____

3.   From chart 3

   a.   In regard to this sacrifice what is the animal to be used?
   _____

   b.   Under the general heading of sheep or goat what are the two
        classes or kinds? _____

   c.   Are these specific in relation to the class or kind?_____

   d.   Did God allow the use of any sheep or goat?_____

   e.   How did God make known his choice? _____
        _____

   f.   Under the general class of sheep or goat there are listed eight
        kinds. Would any of these eight be acceptable as a sacrifice?
        _____
        If not, why not?_____
        _____

   g.   Pick out the specific kind of animal for this sacrifice._____

   h.   Can you see how this excludes the other seven kinds within
        this general realm ? _____

   i.   Suppose one man reasoned: I do not have any male sheep, but
        I have a nice female of the first year, without blemish. Would
        this be alright? _____

   j.   What if a man had no male of the first year, but did have an
        older one without blemish. Would this be acceptable?_____

4.   From chart 4—music

   a.   What is the generic?_____

   b.   What are the two specifics within this class? _____
        _____

   c.   Does each specific have the same relation to the generic?
        _____

    d. Did God command the generic or a specific?_____

    e. How does the choosing of a specific (singing) differ from choosing the generic (music)? _____

_____

5.   Compare charts 1, 2, and 4

    a. The three generic terms are_____

_____

    b. If God's choosing of a specific kind of wood excluded all other kinds, and God's choosing a specific kind of animal excluded all other kinds of animals, does his choosing of a particular kind of music for worship exclude all other kinds?_____

6.   Charts 5—vocal music

    a. Under the general heading of vocal music, name some kinds.

_____

_____

    b. Does each kind bear the same relation to the general heading of vocal music? _____

    c. Did God specify a particular kind of vocal music? _____ What kind? _____

    d. Does this exclude other kinds of vocal music? _____

    e. Under the heading of singing, there are some specifics. Name them._____

_____

    f. Do each of these have the same relation to singing?_____

    g. Explain the difference between this specific and the general term of vocal music._____

_____

7.   Study chart 6

   a.   In studying generic and specific, can you see that animal is generic and sheep is a specific? _____

   b.   Can you see that male and female are specifics under sheep?
   _____

   c.   This means that sheep is a specific in its relation to animal, but there is generic with regard to male and female.

   d.   There are four categories of male sheep. Name them._____
   _____

   e.   There are also four categories of female sheep. Name them.
   _____

   f.   What kind of male sheep did God choose?_____

   g.   This is a specific kind of male, which is a specific of sheep, which is a specific of animal. Would you say God had a choice?
   _____

   h.   Can you see how this kind of male sheep excludes all other kinds of male sheep?_____

   i.   Can you see how this excludes all other kinds of animals?
   _____

8.   Study chart 7

   a.   In studying generic and specific can you see that music is the generic and vocal music is a specific? _____

   b.   Is mechanical instrumental music another kind of music?_____

   c.   Are humming, whistling, yodeling and singing all specific in relation to the generic music?_____

   d.   The chart shows four specifics of singing. What are they?
   _____
   _____

e. What kind of vocal music did God choose?_____

f. Can you see that singing is specific in regard to vocal music, but that it is general in regard to soprano, alto, tenor, or bass?

_____

g. Has God specified whether we sing in soprano, alto, tenor or bass? _____

h. Can you see that singing is a specific kind of vocal music and vocal music is a specific kind of music?_____

 MEMORY—"THY WORD HAVE I HID IN MINE HEART"

1. "Speaking to yourselves in psalms and hymns and spiritual songs, singing and making melody in your heart to the Lord" (Ephesians 5:19).

2. "Saying, I will declare thy name unto my brethren, in the midst of the church will I sing praise unto thee" (Hebrews 2:12).

Singing Praise Unto God

INTRODUCTION

1. A series of lessons on worship would not be complete without a lesson on singing in worship.

    a. Singing is not mentioned with the other acts of worship in Acts 2:32, but is elsewhere commanded (Ephesians 5:19).

    b. This does not mean that the early disciples did not sing before the first mention of singing in the letters to the churches.

    c. The day upon which they broke bread is not mentioned for many years after the establishment of the church, but this does not mean they met on some other day until Acts 20:7.

I. The practice of singing praises unto God

    A. Singing praises unto God is an age old practice of the people of God, a practice that existed long before the beginning of the church.

        1. Moses and Israel sung praises (Exodus 15:1-2; Numbers 21:17).

        2. Deborah the judge sang praises (Judges 5:3).

        3. David the sweet singer of Israel (Psalm 30:4 and many other references).

        4. Isaiah taught Israel to sing praises (Isaiah 12:1, 4).

        5. Jeremiah taught Israel to sing (Jeremiah 20:13).

        6. Ezra and Nehemiah wrote of the singers (Ezra 2:41, 70; Nehemiah 12:42-47).

        7. Jesus and the disciples sung (Matthew 26:30).

    B. The apostles taught the early church to sing. Remember, they were to teach those whom they baptized "to observe all things" Jesus had commanded them (Matthew 28:20).

        1. As a congregation

            a. "in the midst of the church will I sing praises..." (Hebrews 2:12)

       b.   Singing in the church at Corinth (1 Corinthians 14:15).

    2.   As individuals

       a.   Paul and Silas were singing (Acts 16:25).

       b.   "Is any merry? Let him sing psalms" (James 5:13).

II.   The purpose of singing—why should we sing?

(Note: We have reference to singing in worship. We may sing elsewhere and for other purposes, but this is not a study of that kind of singing.)

  A.   It is a command of God that we sing (Ephesians 5:19).

    1.   Because we love God we keep his commandments (1 John 5:3).

    2.   We should sing if we had no other reason but this.

  B.   We like to sing, we enjoy it.

    1.   While it is true that many like to sing, some do not like to sing.

    2.   We do not sing in worship just because we like to sing.

       a.   Our "likes" or "dislikes" do not authorize or condemn anything.

       b.   What of others who say "We like instruments of music" or "We like dancing and clapping of hands." Does this authorize their practice?

  C.   That which is accomplished in singing—why we sing in worship.

    1.   To praise God.

       a.   "In the midst of the church will I sing praises unto thee" (Hebrews 2:12).

       b.   Singing and making melody "to the Lord" (Ephesians 5:19; Colossians 3:16).

    2.   To express joy.

       a.   "Is any merry? let him sing psalms" (James 5:13).

       b.   "Be filled with the Spirit; speaking to yourselves..." (Ephesians 5:18-19)

    3.   To teach and admonish one another.

       a.   "Teaching and admonishing one another with psalms..." (Colossians 3:16)

      b. Note: The songs we sing must teach only the truth.

   4. To speak to ourselves.

      a. "Speaking to yourselves in psalms and hymns…" (Ephesians 5:19)

      b. We are to teach ourselves as well as others.

      Note: Singing is the only kind of music that fulfills the purpose of music in Christian worship.

      Illustration: I attended a funeral recently. I arrived 20 minutes early in order to get a seat. During that 20 minutes organ music was heard throughout the chapel. I did not recognize any tune that was played. There was no teaching, admonishing or edifying by that music.

III.   The requirements for singing

   A. The command is "singing" and a command authorizes everything that is necessary to carrying out that command.

     1. Illustrate:

      a. "Go" into all the world authorizes any kind of going, i.e. any mode of transportation.

      b. "Baptize" authorizes any place where a sufficient amount of water is contained, i.e. river, lake, pond, baptistery.

      c. "Sing" authorizes whatever is required to fulfill the command.

     2. A command authorizes only that which is commanded.

      a. The command "Go" does not authorize a missionary society to do the going or sending.

      b. "Baptize" does not authorize "sprinkling" for baptism.

      c. "Sing" does not authorize any other kind of music.

   B. Singing requires:

     1. A song.

      a. God has specified the kinds of songs for worship, i.e., psalms, hymns, and spiritual songs. There are many good songs which we may sing but which are not suited for worship.

      b. This song may be memorized or written. When written

we have nothing but a song. This authorizes a song book.

    2.   A melody or tune.

        a.   A song would not be a song if there were no melody.

        b.   A song is poetry put to music; if the music (melody) were left off, it would only be poetry.

           (1) Read Psalm 23. That is poetry.

           (2) Sing Psalm 23. That is a song—same words but with a melody.

        c.   The melody may be memorized or written. When written we have only a song. This is authority for a songbook with musical notes.

    3.   A pitch.

        a.   "Pitch" is the highness or lowness of a musical tone.

        b.   It is impossible to sing a song without a pitch. One may sing with the wrong pitch, but one must have a pitch.

        c.   The pitch may be obtained by memory or skill, or by a pitch pipe. This is authority for a pitch pipe to obtain the pitch if necessary.

    4.   A song leader.

        a.   To conduct the singing "decently and in order" (1 Corinthians 14:40) someone must start the song or give a signal when all are to begin. Thus, there is authority for a song leader.

Note: When we sing using a songbook, which contains written words and musical notes, with a song leader, who uses a pitch pipe to obtain the pitch to direct us, we are still doing only that which God commanded—**singing**. We have added nothing to the command.

IV.   The New Testament teaching on music in worship

   A.   Music in worship is found ten times in the New Testament.

      1.   "They had **sung** a hymn..." (Matthew 26:30)

      2.   "They had **sung** a hymn..." (Mark 14:26)

      3.   "Were **singing** hymns unto God" (Acts 16:25).

      4.   "And **sing** unto thy name" (Romans 15:9).

5. "I will **sing** with the spirit..." (1 Corinthians 14:15)

6. "I will **sing** with the understanding also" (1 Corinthians 14:15).

7. "**Singing** and making melody in your heart..." (Ephesians 5:19)

8. "**Singing** with grace in your hearts to the Lord" (Colossians 3:16).

9. "In the midst of the church will I **sing** praise unto thee" (Hebrews 2:12).

10. "Is any merry? let him **sing** psalms" (James 5:13).

B. Singing in worship is restricted to psalms, hymns and spiritual songs. Discuss these terms.

1. Psalms: "Psalms are songs devoted to the praise of God, extolling his name, power, character, and works. The songs of David are mainly of this character, hence were called Psalms" (David Lipscomb, *Commentary on Ephesians*).

   a. "The Psalms are called, in general 'hymns' by Philo; Josephus calls them 'songs and hymns'" (W. E. Vine).

2. Hymns: "Hymns are songs of praise, thanksgiving, and supplication, teaching our dependence on God and his willingness to hear and bless" (Lipscomb, Ibid.).

3. Spiritual songs: "Ode was the generic term for a song, hence the adjective 'spiritual'" (W. E. Vine).

Note: "It is difficult to draw the distinction between songs described as psalms, hymns and spiritual songs. The difficulty arises from the fact that while each term originally denoted a distinct and separate kind of song, frequently two, or even the three distinct kinds sometimes, were combined in one song, and the term came to be used interchangeably" (Lipscomb, Ibid.).

C. God has specified that the "singing and making melody" be "with the heart" (Colossians 3:16; Ephesians 5:19).

1. The human voice—vocal chords—makes the sweetest harmony and melody that is known, and in our worship we are to do this "with the heart" to the Lord.

D. How should we sing:

1. "In spirit" (John 4:23-24)

    a.   Paul said "I will sing with the spirit and with the understanding" (1 Corinthians 14:15).

    b.   "Be filled with the Spirit; speaking to yourselves in psalms and hymns and spiritual songs…" (Ephesians 5:18-19)

    c.   Singing, like all other acts of worship, must be sincere.

2.   "In truth" (John 4:23-24)

    a.   Our songs must teach only the truth (1 Corinthians 14:15). "With the understanding also." We must understand what we sing, and what we sing must not teach something different than the truth.

CONCLUSION

1.   Let us build in our hearts a love for worshipping our God, and like David of old we can say, "My mouth shall praise thee with joyful lips" (Psalm 63:5).

2.   May we with gladness in our hearts sing "psalms and hymns and spiritual songs" unto our God, knowing that "singing and making melody in our heart to the Lord" is the kind of music our Father in heaven desires.

3.   To the children of God, and to the Father in heaven and our Lord Jesus Christ, there is no sweeter music under heaven than "the fruit of our lips" as "in the midst of the church" we sing praises unto our God.

> "O for a thousand tongues to sing
> My great Redeemer's praise,
> The glories of my God and King,
> The triumphs of his grace!"

> "Praise ye the Lord, Praise the Lord,
> O my soul.
> While I live will I praise the Lord:
> I will sing praises unto my God
> while I have any being."
> (Psalm 146:1-2)

> "Praise ye the Lord: for it is good to
> sing praises unto our God;
> for it is pleasant; and praise is comely."
> (Psalm 147:1)

Some Questions About Singing

WHAT DOES THE SCRIPTURE SAY?

References: Exodus 15:1-2; Judges 5:3; Psalm 30:4; Isaiah 12:1;
Jeremiah 20:13; Ezra 2:41, 70; Nehemiah 12:42-47; Matthew 26:30;
Mark 14:26; Acts 16:25; Romans 15:9; 1 Corinthians 14:15; Ephesians 5:19;
Colossians 3:16; Hebrews 2:12; James 5:13

1.   "Then _____ Moses and the children of Israel this
     _____ unto the Lord, and spake, saying, I will _____
     unto the Lord, for he hath triumphed gloriously..."

2.   "Hear, O ye kings; give ear, O ye princes; I even I, will _____
     _____ unto the Lord: I will _____ _____ to the
     Lord God of Israel."

3.   "_____ unto the Lord, O ye _____ of his, and give
     _____ at the remembrance of his holiness."

4.   "And in that day shall ye say, _____ the Lord, _____
     upon his name, declare his doings among the people, make
     mention that his name is _____."

5.   "Sing unto the _____, praise ye the Lord; for he hath
     _____ the soul of the poor form the hand of evil doers."

6.   "The _____: the _____ of Asaph, a hundred twenty
     and eight."

7.   "For in the days of David and Asaph of old there were chief of the
     _____, and songs of _____ and _____ unto
     God."

8.   "And when they had _____ a _____, they went out into
     the mount of Olives."

9. "And when they had _____ a _____, they went out into the mount of Olives."

10. "And at midnight Paul and Silas _____, and _____ praises unto _____: and the prisoners heard them."

11. "And that the Gentiles might _____ God for his mercy: as it is written, For this cause I will _____ to thee among the Gentiles, and _____ unto thy name."

12. "...I will _____ with the _____ and I will _____ with the understanding also."

13. "Speaking to yourselves in _____ and _____ and _____ _____, singing and making _____ in your heart to the Lord."

14. "...Teaching and admonishing one another in _____ and _____ and _____ _____, singing with _____ in your heart to the Lord."

15. "Saying, I will _____ thy name unto my brethren, in the midst of the church will I _____ _____ unto thee."

16. "Is any among you _____? let him _____. Is any _____? let him _____ psalms."

BRIEF ANSWERS

1. What is a song? _____
   _____

2. What is singing? _____
   _____

3. What does it mean to "praise"? _____
   _____

4. Why do we sing in worship? _____
   _____

5. Is singing in worship restricted to particular kinds of songs?

    _____

 TALK TIME—DISCUSSION

1. Discuss the practice of singing in O.T. days.

    a. What is the earliest reference you can find to singing praises to God? _____

    b. Which of the judges said, "I will sing praise to the Lord God of Israel"? _____

    c. Name some of the prophets who taught the people of Israel to sing. _____

    _____

2. The apostles taught people to sing praises unto God.

    a. Give a reference which shows that the church is to sing.

    _____

    b. Do we have an example of the apostles singing?_____
        Give a reference. _____

3. How do we know that Jesus approved of singing praises and engaged in such? _____

    There are two references which show us that Jesus sung hymns. What are they? _____

4. There are at least five reasons why Christians should sing. List these reasons and give a reference for each.

    a. _____

    b. _____

    c. _____

    d. _____

    e. _____

5.   Tell the class what it means to praise God, and name a song which we sing to praise God. _____

_____

_____

6.   Songs often express the joy we feel in our hearts. Name a psalm or song which expresses joy. _____

_____

7.   We are to teach and admonish one another in the songs we sing. Select a song which illustrates this. _____

_____

8.   What does the expression "Speaking to yourselves" mean (Ephesians 5:19)? _____

_____

9.   What are the requirements for singing?

a.   _____

b.   _____

c.   _____

d.   _____

10.   What kind of songs are to be sung in worship? _____

_____

11.   Discuss the meaning of:

a.   psalms _____

_____

b.   hymns _____

_____

c.   spiritual songs _____

_____

12. Why is it often difficult to distinguish between psalms, hymns and spiritual songs?_____

_____

13. Singing, like all other true worship, must be rendered "in spirit and in truth."

   a. What does it mean to sing "in spirit"? _____

   _____

   b. What does it mean to sing "in truth"? _____

   _____

THINK! "THINK ON THESE THINGS"

1. Some say we sing because we like it.

   a. It is true that many Christians like to sing, but does the fact that we like to sing authorize the practice? THINK!_____

   _____

   b. Is it right for one who doesn't like to sing to just refuse to sing? THINK! _____

   c. Do we obey the commandments of the Lord only when we like it? THINK! _____

   d. What about one who says, "I can't carry a tune"? THINK!

   _____

   e. Does God expect the impossible of anyone? THINK! _____

2. If one really cannot sing what should he do during the song service? THINK!_____

   _____

   a. Should he talk to those beside him? THINK!_____
      Why not? THINK! _____

   _____

   b. Should he entertain the babies? THINK!_____

    c. Should he follow along reading the words and trying to understand the lessons taught? THINK!_____

3.   What about a person who is "dumb" and cannot sing? THINK!

_____

What should he do? THINK! _____

_____

4.   In the outline we studied the purpose of singing (to obey God, to praise God, to express joy, to teach one another, and to speak unto ourselves).

    a. Was there ever a time when men were to praise God by playing upon an instrument (Psalm 150)? THINK! _____

    b. Can instrumental music express joy? THINK!_____

    c. Can we teach one another the word of God by playing on an instrument? THINK! _____

    d. Is it possible to "speak to yourself" by playing an instrument? THINK! _____

5.   A command authorizes everything that is necessary to carry out that which is commanded.

    a. Does the command to "sing" authorize a song? THINK! _____

    b. Are we free to choose any song we like? THINK! _____

    c. What restricts the kinds of songs we are to sing in worship? THINK! _____

        _____

    d. Where does the choice of songs fit into the command to sing? THINK! _____

        _____

6.   Do some thinking about the melody.

    a. Is it possible to sing a song without a tune or melody? THINK!

        _____

   b. Has God commanded which melody to use? THINK! _____

   c. Who arranges and writes the melody for the songs we sing in worship? THINK! _____
Is this authorized? THINK!_____
Who writes the words of the songs we sing? THINK! _____

_____

7.   Thinking about song books.

   a. Is it necessary to have a song book? THINK! _____

   b. How could we sing without a song book? THINK! _____

   c. Why do we use song books? THINK! _____

_____

   d. When we use songbooks which contain a selection of psalms, hymns and spiritual songs, and we sing one of these songs, are we doing what the Lord commanded? THINK! _____

8.   It is a common practice among brethren to have a "song leader." Let's do some thinking about the song leader.

   a. Is he singing "for" us? THINK!_____

   b. Is he singing to entertain the assembly? THINK! _____

   c. What is the purpose of a song leader or director? THINK!

_____

_____

   d. When we sing with a song leader are we doing what God has commanded? THINK! _____
Are we "adding to" what he has commanded? THINK! _____

9.   Do some thinking about getting the "pitch".

   a. What is a "pitch"? THINK!_____

_____

   b. Can we sing without a pitch? THINK! _____

    c.   Has God told us how to get the pitch? THINK! _____

    d.   What are some ways of getting the pitch? THINK!_____

        _____

    e.   What is a "pitch pipe" or a "tuning fork"? THINK! _____

        _____

    f.   What is the purpose of a pitch pipe? THINK! _____

        _____

    g.   When a song leader uses a pitch pipe to obtain the pitch for a song and the congregation sings the song beginning with that pitch, are we doing **what** God has commanded? THINK! _____ Are we doing more than he has commanded? THINK! _____

10.   We are to sing "in spirit and in truth." Think about this for a minute.

    a.   If some are talking during the song service are they singing in spirit? THINK!_____

    b.   If instead of singing we are thinking about what we are to do after the service, are we worshipping "in spirit"? THINK!

        _____

    c.   If we sing a song that does not teach the truth, can we sing it "in truth"? THINK! _____

    d.   Can you see why brethren select song books that have been edited by a Christian? THINK! _____

    e.   When some are late in arriving at the meeting place and the worship has begun, what is best for them to do? THINK!

        _____

        If brethren are praying should they wait until the prayer has ended then enter the auditorium, or should they go right in and find a seat while the church is praying unto God? THINK!

        _____

        If brethren are singing should they wait until the song is ended before entering? THINK!_____

WHAT YOU SHOULD LEARN FROM THIS LESSON

1. Christians are to worship God in song.

2. We are to sing psalms, hymns, and spiritual songs.

3. Our singing is to praise God, express joy, to teach and admonish one another and to speak unto ourselves.

4. The songs may be memorized or written in a book and the pitch may be obtained by skill, memory, or a pitch pipe.

5. We must sing "in spirit and in truth" to worship as true worshippers.

"Praise ye the Lord.
Praise ye the Lord from the heavens; praise him in the heights.
Praise ye him, all his angels: praise ye him, all his hosts.
Praise ye him, sun and moon: praise him, all ye stars of light.
Praise him, ye heavens of heavens,
and ye waters that be above the heavens,
Let them praise the name of the Lord:
for he commanded, and they were created.
He hath also stablished them for ever and ever:
he hath made a decree which shall not pass.

Praise the Lord from the earth, ye dragons, and all deeps:
Fire, and hail; snow and vapour; stormy wind fulfilling his word:
Mountains, and all hills; fruitful trees, and all cedars:
Beasts, and all cattle; creeping things, and flying fowl:
Kings of the earth, and all people; princes, and all judges of the earth;
Both young men, and maidens; old men, and children:
Let them praise the name of the Lord, for his name alone is excellent;
his glory is above the earth and heaven."
(Psalm 148:1-13)

Made in the USA
Columbia, SC
16 May 2023

16800415R10085